MARK H. M^cCORMACK
ON NEGOTIATING

DOVE
BOOKS

ISBN 0-7871-0295-4

Printed in the United States of America

Dove Books
301 North Cañon Drive
Beverly Hills, CA 90210

Distributed by Penguin USA

Text design and layout by Frank Loose Design
Jacket design by Rick Penn-Kraus
Photo of Mark H. McCormack courtesy of Berliner Studios

First Printing: September 1995

10 9 8 7 6 5 4 3 2 1

ON NEGOTIATING

Contents

CHAPTER 6

CHAPTER 7

INDEX

ON NEGOTIATING

Only Man Negotiates

I'm not sure what private language dolphins, chimpanzees, and wildebeests use to settle their differences. It's quite possible that every living thing has a secret tongue for communicating offers and counteroffers, for asking questions that reveal what something is truly worth, for splitting the difference, for highballing or lowballing, for deflecting objections and turning them into advantages—indeed for executing every strategem you'll find in this book.

But only man has formalized the negotiating process to the nth degree. (What other creature uses deal memos, confirmation letters, and contracts to seal a negotiation?)

Only man negotiates as an alternative to the use of brute force. (To all other creatures, brute force is the essence of negotiating.)

Only man creates rules and procedures for how we should talk to each other when we want what someone else has. (I doubt if even the highest nonhuman life-forms worry too much about seating arrangements, order of speaking, and who writes the first draft.)

My purpose in writing this book is not to glorify businessmen and -women as negotiators. It's not to extol the sophisticated extremes to which all of us are capable of going in order to settle our differences.

On the contrary, if I can impart one message, it is that negotiating in business is often more complicated than it has to be. We make it so—by insisting that everyone follow certain rules, by believing outdated assumptions, by overthinking the other side's position or adhering too tightly to ours, and most obviously, by putting too much faith in "conventional wisdom" (whatever that means!).

A friend once introduced me to a college audience I was invited to by saying, "It's easy to understand the advice Mr. McCormack is about to give you if you realize that he starts with the premise that *everything you know is wrong!*"

I'm not sure my friend was 100 percent correct, but I appreciated the sentiment. I'm not a contrarian by nature, nor a rebel for the sake of being rebellious, nor a negotiating sociopath who flouts convention and politesse. (Actually, you'll discover this book places a high premium on the most traditional value of all: In the end, every negotiating decision must be guided by the Golden Rule—to do unto others as you would have them do unto you.)

But I do think that a lot of what passes for "shrewd" or "gutsy" negotiating these days is nothing more than boilerplate responses to situations that we think we have seen and dealt with before. I prefer to think that every negotiating situation, no matter how much déjà vu it inspires, is in some sense new and unfamiliar. Identifying the new elements is what keeps negotiating from ever becoming stale or predictable for me. It demands a response that is unconventional, even if only by a few degrees. In that sense, I guess I am guilty of believing that "everything you know is wrong." I remind myself of that every day. The "you" applies to me more than anyone else.

Two Recurring Themes

One of the two recurring themes you'll find in this primer is *question everything*. I advocate a healthy skepticism to any rules, numbers, and assumptions in a negotiation. This is the appropriate response to the fact that, despite superficial evidence to the contrary, no two negotiations are the same. What you applied two weeks ago won't work today. There's a lot to be said for consistency in business, but not in negotiating. Consistency makes you predictable. Being predictable means a sharp-eyed adversary can discern your style. And having a particular style or pattern can often work against you.

The other recurring theme is *think big*. I intend to exhort people to shoot for the moon on every major deal point. Just as most people take comfort in negotiations that seem familiar, most people, in my opinion, are overly fond of taking monetary and nonmonetary positions that fall down the middle. Extreme positions, whether it means quoting an "outrageously" high price or making an offer that is "insultingly" low, make them uncomfortable. But negotiating down the middle is splitting the difference, which even four-year-olds can do. It requires a very modest skill set for a negotiator (and you won't learn it here). If you have to boil down your negotiating attitude to two things, you can do a lot worse than *question everything* and *think big*.

3

WHERE I'M COMING FROM

You may rightfully ask who I am to pontificate on negotiating. I am not a seminarist on the art of negotiating. I don't conduct all-day programs in hotel ballrooms where I list "32 ways to achieve closure" on an overhead projector or divide the audience into small groups as I put them through their paces in mock negotiating situations.

Nor do I negotiate multibillion-dollar corporate mergers and financial deals, the kind you read about on the front pages of the newspaper. Those megadeals seem slightly surreal to me. When negotiators blithely raise their bid by $750 million or $1 billion, they're dealing in a currency I have a hard time relating to. I can't help thinking they're negotiating with play money, usually borrowed from a bank or provided by shareholders. I'd be much more impressed if the money came out of the negotiators' own pockets.

My sole negotiating credential is that I run a sports marketing company, which I started 35 years ago in Cleveland, Ohio, with $500 in capital, called International Management Group.

We represent hundreds of well-known athletes such as Arnold Palmer (my first client), Jackie Stewart, Jean-Claude Killy, Bjorn Borg, Chris Evert, Alberto Tomba, and Andre Agassi. In recent years, we have branched out into the representation of classical musicians and singers such as Itzhak Perlman, James Galway, and Kiri Te Kanawa.

We create and manage events, everything from the Toyota World Match Play at Wentworth to a José Carreras concert in Singapore to the Detroit Grand Prix motor race to *Jesus Christ Superstar* in Sydney to the Dubai Snooker Classic. We represent the Nobel Foundation. We have helped develop the commercial interests of Wimbledon and the Royal and Ancient Golf Club of St. Andrews.

Our television arm, Trans World International, has represented the international broadcast rights for sports properties such as the Olympic Games, the World and European Figure Skating championships, the National Football League, all the major golf and tennis championships, and the 24 Hours of Le Mans. It is also the world's largest independent producer of television sports programming.

I have negotiated personal services and endorsement deals for our clients on every continent. As our company has grown, I've also negotiated with real estate people about more office space in London, with employees about their compensation, and with inscrutable Japanese television executives about sports programming. In almost every case, whether the sum involved is £1,000 or $400 million, I've regarded the stakes as enormous—because I'm dealing with my client's money or my own. In 1984 when I wrote my first book, *What They Don't Teach You at Harvard Business School*, IMG had 500 employees in 19 offices around the world generating several hundred million dollars in revenue. Today we have nearly 2,000 employees and 69 offices in 28 countries, and revenues have surged well beyond the billion-dollar mark. We obviously have conducted a few successful negotiations in the interval.

Before I started writing *On Negotiating*, I surveyed the competition. The good books on the subject opened my eyes to a whole new world of negotiating jargon such as BATNA (the Best Alternative To a Negotiated Agreement) and "bogey" (which I always thought was one stroke over par but, to negotiating theorists, is any imaginary device used to threaten the other side). The books were loaded with hypothetical situations, clever expansions on game theory, dramatic stories clipped from magazines and newspapers, and fables that rang with wisdom.

The cutest story I ran across (from William Ury's breezy but useful *Getting Past No*) tells about a man who left 17 camels to his three sons. He left half the camels to his eldest son, a third to his middle son, and a ninth to his youngest. When the three sons tried to divide up their inheritance, they couldn't negotiate a solution because 17 was not divisible by two, three, or nine. The sons consulted a wise old woman who told them, "See what happens if you take my camel." That gave the sons 18 camels. The oldest son took his half, i.e., nine camels. The middle son took his third, or six camels. The youngest took a ninth, or two camels. Nine and six and two made 17. They had one camel left over, which they returned to the old woman.

As I say, it's a cute reminder about the benefits of looking at a situation from a different angle. The only problem is I've never negotiated for camels and don't know anyone else in the dromedary trade. Splitting the inheritance into halves, thirds, and ninths also sounds like a tortured contrivance— more a math riddle than a negotiating principle you can act on.

The negotiating examples you'll read herein have all involved me or our company in some way. They're not fables or hypotheticals or clippings from a faded newspaper. They're real. In some cases, our side comes out the hero. In others, we look less than brilliant (I cite them so you can learn from my mistakes).

THREE CAVEATS ABOUT THIS BOOK

First, I should explain the difference between *negotiating* and *selling*. As any salesperson knows, there's an extremely fine line between selling and negotiating. In many situations, there is no line at all. You're negotiating terms for your product or service at the same time you are trying to generate interest in that product or service. The customer is intrigued at one price, indifferent at another. Is the process of making the customer's interest and your price meet called selling or negotiating? It's hard to say. For the purposes of this primer, let us agree that negotiating is the end game of the sales process. Selling is the process of identifying customers, then getting through to them, then increasing their awareness and interest in your product or service, and finally persuading them to act on that interest. (I cover this in a companion volume, *On Selling*.) Negotiating is the process of getting the best terms once the other side starts to act on their interest.

Second, there are two sides to any negotiation: the seller's and the buyer's. Because I sell for a living, you'll find a heavy emphasis on the selling side of negotiation here. It's not because I think the buying side is less important. But I do think there is more urgency to selling. If you're a buyer, you can always walk away from a negotiation and wait for another day. A seller doesn't have that luxury. A seller who does nothing but walk away will eventually go out of business.

Third, I've sometimes described my earlier books as "popcorn." They're like a bag of popcorn because you can dip in anywhere and find a morsel to chew on. This book is different. It begins with the elementary tools of negotiating and leads you steadily to increasingly advanced techniques. It's meant to be read from beginning to end. Of course, you could turn to page 183 and read how we set up a record-breaking auction in Scotland. But the strategies we employed in that negotiation will have a more lasting impact if you've mastered the material that came before. With those caveats in mind, let's get started.

CHAPTER 1

How Anyone Can Outnegotiate Me

I've been saying for years that to be the perfect negotiator, you need the following personal skills in your briefcase:

- **Perfect people sense:** Knowing what makes people tick and how far you can push your position before the other side resists or resents it.

- **A strong competitive streak:** Enjoying the hand-to-hand combat that is the essence of negotiating.

- **A wide field of vision:** Seeing the big picture, the long-term consequences as well as the short-term gains.

- **An eye for details:** Being able to spot the thorny issue that everyone else overlooks in a transaction.

- **Unimpeachable integrity:** Meaning what you say. You don't have to be hounded to keep your promises.

It's interesting to me that, as much as I prize these qualities in a negotiator, only one of the above attributes would be particularly effective in a negotiating session with me.

A negotiator could have faultless people sense with others, but I try to be inscrutable in a negotiation. I don't reveal much in terms of information or inclination (unless it's intentional), so perfect people pitch might not work so well with me.

Likewise with a strong competitive streak. I respect that quality in others, and it probably alerts me to be more competitive as well. The two cancel each other out.

I also like dealing with people who see the big picture. Quite often, the fact that they can see long-term allows me to negotiate new features into our transaction, the kind of features that the other side recognizes as beneficial in the long run.

Although I'm impressed with people who have an eye for details, I tend to deal in broad strokes in most negotiations. The details often don't grab my attention, nor do the people who harp on them. (I'm not bragging; this is surely a weakness on my part.)

The one quality in the list above that does work on me, however, is unimpeachable integrity. If I'm convinced of the other side's sense of honor and fair play, I'll usually let them get away with negotiating points that I would fight over with more slippery people.

(In much the same vein, I'm also a soft touch with genuinely nice people. Although niceness is not traditionally regarded as a negotiating skill [toughness is], it does have an effect on me. Rather than walk all over the nice negotiator, I tend to get nicer myself—and yield more often than I should.)

The real secret to outnegotiating me (and most other people as well) can be summed up in one word: knowledge. If you know something about me or our company that I don't want you to know, you have a tremendous negotiating edge.

Here are four examples of knowledge that I would prefer you didn't have.

1. THE CLIENT NEEDS THE MONEY.

In our company, we're usually negotiating for a client, not for ourselves. We commission a percentage of the monies we secure, but the bulk of the money goes to the client. We don't sign the contracts we negotiate; the client does. In other words, no matter how involved we are in a negotiation, the client is the decision maker.

A lot of people on the other side of the table don't fully appreciate that. After weeks or months of dealing with us in person or over the phone on all the fine points of, say, a shoe contract for a superstar athlete, they forget that we are just the agent. They think we have total control over the life or death of the deal. In truth, we don't. We're obliged to go back to the athlete, make our recommendation, and let him or her decide. Sometimes clients listen to us. Sometimes they don't.

A negotiator who fully appreciates that dynamic has a leg up on someone who doesn't.

A negotiator who appreciates that dynamic *and* knows something about our client's personal affairs probably has a leg up on us.

For example, let's say the other side knows or even suspects that our client has suffered a financial setback. The setback could be the result of an injury that limited his or her on-the-field income, a messy divorce, a bad investment, or any number of things. Given the media attention devoted to our athlete clients, this sort of intelligence is not hard to obtain. But the bottom line is: The client needs money.

That's the worst sort of client to negotiate for. A client desperate for money makes desperate decisions. If the other side gets the slightest whiff of that, they can outnegotiate me.

2. I NEED A DEAL TO KEEP A THIRD PARTY HAPPY.

Money isn't the only factor that makes clients desperate. Sometimes it's the nagging suspicion that their peers are getting better contracts that makes them unhappy.

We see this more often than we like in our business. Let's say an athlete is perfectly happy with the job we've done for him. Then he reads in the press that a perceived rival has signed a large endorsement contract. Suddenly a happy client becomes unhappy. He wants to know why we aren't doing the same for him. He makes some rumbling noises about seeking other representation. It's not necessarily rational, but it's understandable. Clients switch management all the time, often for the flimsiest reasons. It's a dangerous mix of "The other man's grass is always greener" and "What have you done for me lately?"

To keep the client, we might have to drum up a contract that salves his bruised ego. We have to prove what we have done lately. In other words, we (not the client) are desperate.

That's a lousy negotiating posture to be in. If the other side somehow knows (a) what the client is feeling and (b) that I have to make a deal—any deal—to soothe the disgruntled client, they can outnegotiate me.

3. I'M OBSESSED WITH THE IDEA.

As a general rule, I like to be objective about the product or services I'm selling in a negotiation. I have a fixed number in my head as to the value of the product or service. If I can remain objective, I'm more likely to stick to my number and walk away when I see the other side is too far away.

But like most people, I have pet projects that I either conceived or have adopted as my own. I have a fixed value in my head with these as well. But it's hard to be objective with my favorites. I'd rather see them come to life, even if it means leaving some money on the table, than watch them wither away over a deal point.

Obviously, I do my best to keep these pet projects to myself. If the other side knows that I'm obsessed with an idea, they can outnegotiate me.

4. I DON'T WANT MY COMPETITORS TO GET IT.

Most businesses have a clear idea of what market share is in their industry. If you're AT&T, you know how much of the long-distance telephone market you control. And you'll do anything to protect that market share from competitors like MCI or Sprint. You'll sweeten deals with current customers to keep them from switching to the competition. You might give rebates to induce MCI or Sprint customers to switch to you. If customers are aware of that, if they know how vital market share is in your scheme of things, they can negotiate a better deal for themselves.

Market share is not so clear-cut in our business. It's more a state of mind, which is how I like it. Few people really know

13

how many of the world's top athletes we manage in a particular sport or how many of the world's top sports events we represent. And no one really knows whether or not we are satisfied with our "market share" or whether we will do anything to increase it.

If they knew how we really felt about our competition, they could outnegotiate me.

CHAPTER 2

The Tools at Your Disposal

WHAT IS TALENT IN A NEGOTIATOR?

Most coaches have a good idea of what constitutes talent in an athlete. They look for the basics of speed, strength, endurance, eye-hand coordination, grace, quick reflexes. After that they look for the rarer qualities of a champion: durability, perfect eyesight, and intangibles such as self-confidence, mental toughness, and killer instinct. Even a marginally alert sports fan can spot raw athletic talent.

It's not much different for bosses scouting for negotiating talent. You just need an eye for the right attributes. A talented negotiator is someone who:

1. DOESN'T NEED TO BE LIKED

There's a difference between being liked by the other side and needing to be liked.

Getting others to like you because of your brains, charm, honesty, or sense of humor is a strength. When the other side can go either way on an issue, they're more likely to yield to you if they like you.

Needing to be liked is a weakness, especially if satisfying that need compels you to sacrifice negotiating points. People who need to be liked are easily seduced. They'd rather leave money on the table than risk offending the other side. Talented negotiators never let personal friendships affect their firmness on an issue. They know it's just business.

Who would you rather have negotiating on your behalf—someone who doesn't care what the other side thinks of him or her or someone who does?

2. CAN TOLERATE AMBIGUITY AND CONFLICT

In golf, Seve Ballesteros is known as a scrambler. He's often wild off the tee, yet he can improvise shots from horrible positions to make birdies or save par. Few pros have his talent for improvisation.

It's the same in negotiating. A lot of people can't cope when the discussion takes a 90-degree turn or the issues on the table veer out of bounds. They're so locked into their position, they don't realize that circumstances can change in the middle of a negotiation and render all previous agreements moot. A talented negotiator knows how to scramble and improvise.

I've been involved in what I thought were unilateral negotiations with another party for one of our client's services when a second and third party tried to inject themselves into the discussion with rival bids. As the client's representative I welcome that sort of "disturbance." Competition always means a better deal for my client.

But sometimes the original party's response has surprised me. Some people, it turns out, can't tolerate this sort of chaos and ambiguity in a negotiation. They can't scramble. Rather than accept the changing landscape of the negotiation and improvise a response, they doggedly stick to their position— and inevitably watch one of their rivals steal the deal away.

3. HAS A LOT OF INTEGRITY

Integrity in a negotiator is like consistency in an athlete. It's not apparent right away and it takes time for other people to appreciate it. But it's a talent nonetheless, because if you are known for your integrity, the other side will be more willing to accommodate you. They might relax on payment terms or let you set aside collateral issues to a more propitious date. If integrity is not your strong suit, you may have trouble getting the other side to come to the table.

4. DOESN'T NEED TO BE THE SMARTEST PERSON IN THE ROOM

The smartest person in the room is not necessarily the best negotiator. In fact, the smartest person may be the worst negotiator, especially if that person thinks he or she has all the answers and, consequently, neglects to ask the right questions.

Before a negotiation I always remind myself to discuss each major point as if I'm starting at ground zero. I don't pretend to be smart in areas I'm not, and I'm willing to appear ignorant in areas where I'm really smart.

If the other side is taking some issues for granted because "it's always been done that way," I challenge the tradition. It's amazing how asking the other side to explain the reasoning behind a standard clause can get you a more favorable, and definitely nonstandard, result.

The beauty of not needing to be the smartest person all the time is that it keeps the other side off balance. They don't know what you actually know, so they often attribute more street smarts to you than you may actually possess.

A college basketball coach once told me about recruiting a high school basketball star in Pennsylvania. After seeing him play an outstanding game in the state championship, the coach visited the young man and his father. The coach explained the limit on full scholarships at his college and offered the young man a partial scholarship. The young man and his father didn't say a word.

Although the coach had negotiated scholarship offers with many shrewd (and grasping) parents and players in his time, the silence unsettled him. He hadn't expected a 17-year-old kid to play hard to get. So he improved his offer to a full scholarship. The coach later learned that the young man's silence was not a negotiating ploy. He was shy and his father was naive. To them the coach's initial offer was so generous, they didn't know what to say.

5. WILL NEGOTIATE ANYTHING

An athlete may have a unique talent for, say, tennis, but if that athlete doesn't love tennis, he or she will never excel at it. The same with negotiators. They may have all the above attributes, but if they don't love to negotiate, they will always be outgunned by someone who does love it.

The best negotiator I know, a super-successful entrepreneur, regards everything as negotiable. He devotes the same enthusiasm and care to negotiating for a wristwatch as he does to negotiating his multimillion-dollar deals. I have dined with him and seen him negotiate the price of an appetizer and entrée. I don't know anybody else who does that. I'm convinced he can't help himself.

But that's the greatest talent for all successful negotiators. For them, negotiating is a sport they love. And like athletes, they do it constantly so they're never out of shape.

A Great Negotiator Needs to Be Great at Only One Thing

I've said in the previous chapter that the perfect negotiator should have:

- Faultless people sense

- A strong competitive streak

- A view of the big picture

- An eye for the crucial detail

- Unimpeachable integrity

What's interesting to me here is that I don't know too many people who have all these qualities, yet I know a lot of great salespeople and negotiators. They're not "perfect" by any means; in many cases, they are just slightly above average in exhibiting the above qualities. But over the years I've noticed that great negotiators have one thing in common: Despite their various shortcomings, each of them has one overriding strength—and knows how to exploit it.

For example, some years ago I found myself conducting business on separate projects with two division heads at a large conglomerate. On paper, these two division heads could not have been more alike. They had the same rank, the same title, and the same number of years at the company, and their divisions were of equal size and generated, more or less, the same profits. Both men had brains, substance, and integrity, which made them potent negotiators.

And yet, over the course of several visits, I found myself gravitating toward one over the other because, in person, he was infinitely more pleasant than the other fellow. He would work *with* me to resolve an issue rather than *against* me. I never got the sense that we were adversaries. In short, his overriding strength as a deal maker was his *likability*. People would tend to want to see him again and again, whereas they might not want repeat visits with his colleague.

Now, likability is hardly the distinguishing mark of a great negotiator. (There are lots of likable people; however, not all of them are skilled negotiators. In fact, their niceness often makes them poor negotiators.) But in this instance, with everything else being equal, this executive's likable character made him first among equals.

The point is, I think all of us have one talent or personality trait that can help us in selling and negotiating. The key is to recognize that quality in ourselves—and let it prevail. Here are four traits, any one of which can turn an average negotiator into a great one.

1. PATIENCE

Patience may be a virtue, but in negotiating it is a weapon of incalculable power. I see this repeatedly in our company. The exercise of patience can turn a mediocre transaction into a great one. The absence of patience can destroy your profit margins.

We once had an executive whose overriding flaw was his impatience. He loved to make deals. He couldn't walk out of a room without a deal. He was constitutionally incapable of waiting for another meeting, even though waiting could have been an advantage. As a result he tended to fold more quickly on price. He would take $10 in order to make a deal rather than wait for $50 or fight for $100. He did a lot of deals, but very few were profitable.

His successor was a welcome change as a negotiator. He wasn't shy about asking for more money, and he wasn't afraid of walking out of the room and waiting for a month. He had the patience to wait for that third or fourth meeting for conditions to improve—and the terms to become more attractive. He didn't close as many deals, but those he did were dramatically more profitable than his predecessor's.

If you can outwait the other side, you can usually out-negotiate them.

2. CLARITY

Some people use confusion as a negotiating tool. They shower the other party with a blizzard of buzzwords and jargon in an effort to dazzle that person. But more likely, they leave the other party confused about what is being agreed upon.

By contrast, there are other people whose chief strength is their ability to express themselves clearly and succinctly. They can outline a concept in a paragraph where others might need two or three pages. They're not classic negotiators in the sense that they're adversarial or trying to impress and intimidate the other side. They're not slick or theatrical. Quite often they don't even think of themselves as salespeople or negotiators. They simply build their case logically and quickly and make things easier to understand. As a result, they end up being much more persuasive and commanding than they imagine.

If you have nothing else going for you but a superior ability to communicate, you can be a superior negotiator.

3. MASTERY OF DETAILS

Quite often in a negotiating session, the most persuasive person in the room is the one who has the greatest expertise and mastery of the details.

For example, there is an executive in our company whom I regard as our secret weapon in almost every corporate marketing transaction. If we are talking to a company about sponsoring, say, a golf tournament, I always make sure he's part of the sales and negotiating team. In a typical sales situation, I often start the ball rolling by suggesting sponsorship of a golf event. One of our sales executives may then elaborate: "Here are all the marketing concepts you can do with a golf tournament. . . ." But as the discussions move along, we've learned that at some point the company's people will want to know how they can tell if their investment in golf is helping them sell more product or reach more customers. That's when this executive steps up to the plate and displays his mastery of the details. He shows the other side how, if they ever run a golf tournament, we have the following 14 ways of evaluating its effectiveness. As he talks about CPMs (cost per thousand), televised impressions, and the other gauges of an event's impact, you can almost see the other side getting excited about the potential impact. They're thinking, "Gee, if we can get all that information out of an event, maybe we should do it!"

Although this executive isn't really selling or negotiating, the bottom line is that without his contribution, the customer probably wouldn't buy.

If your mastery of a specific area is better than anyone else's, your negotiating skills are probably better than theirs too.

4. ADMINISTRATIVE SKILL

Administrative skill is also a negotiating weapon.

For example, another executive at our company is very concerned with administrative details and expenses. He's good at it. He thinks about it a lot. His negotiating style is to find the real dollars in any deal. Where a lesser executive might announce that we'll make $50,000 from a sale without realizing that it will cost us $51,000 to execute it, this particular executive will have our costs firmly established before he ever quotes a price. He uses his administrative expertise and works backward to figure out how aggressive he has to be on price.

If you have a better handle on what things cost than anyone else in the room, that, too, is a negotiating advantage.

What's Minor to You May Be Major to the Other Side

If every negotiation consists of major and minor negotiating points, the biggest irony is that it's usually the minor issues— the technicality, the seemingly innocent clause, the oddball request—that can kill the deal. That's why I always advise our salespeople, deal makers, and attorneys to not only pay close attention to the minor issues in a negotiation but to always question why the other side is insisting on them. The simple act of questioning each minor point can tell you a lot about the other side's intentions and ultimately can save you a lot of trouble.

A few years ago I filmed a video of one of my business books at a new resort in Europe where our company's golf and television divisions had teamed up to create and broadcast a golf tournament. It seemed like a smart, cost-efficient move at the time, since the film crew, the equipment, and I were obliged to be at the resort for several days.

The owner of the resort liked the idea and even agreed to pay us a fee for filming the video on that property. He considered it a good way to promote the resort. In exchange, we would show the resort in an attractive light in the video, mention it in the credits, and provide the resort with 100 free copies of the finished product.

To us, the major issue was receiving a fee to help defray our production costs. To the resort, the major issue was receiving positive exposure in a video that would be seen by thousands of people around the world.

When we prepared the contract, the resort owner inserted a clause requiring us to provide a one-inch master tape of the finished video for his own internal promotional use. It seemed like an odd request. Why would a golf resort want the master tape? What would they do with 60 minutes of me talking? We didn't press the issue. After all, sending a duplicate master would be an easy requirement to fulfill.

We filmed the video, incorporating the required scenic shots of the resort in the final edit, and duly sent off the master tape to our contact there. A few days later the owner called us up. He liked the video but was disappointed by the scenic shots. There simply wasn't enough footage that he could edit out and use in a video to promote his resort.

It turned out that the innocent "master tape" clause was a major issue to him. He was hoping that, during our shoot, we would provide miles of first-class footage of his resort from which he could construct his own professionally shot promotional video.

If we had known that, we would have filmed his resort from every possible angle and provided him with more footage than he would ever need. The cost to us would have been negligible. But we didn't—because nobody asked him why he inserted that seemingly minor negotiating point into the agreement. If we had asked, we would have learned his true agenda and could have done something about it, something that would have further cemented our relationship rather than nearly fracture it.

What should have been a simple, easily executed "win-win" agreement ended on a needlessly sour note. And it was our fault, not his.

Keep this in mind the next time you're in the middle of a negotiation. Don't be so distracted by the major deal points—i.e., the sale price, the payment terms, your fee—that you ignore the minor deal points that seem harmless or merely weird at the time. There are no red flags flying over the minor points, warning you to examine them carefully, but quite often there should be.

HOLD YOUR FIRE WHEN THE OTHER SIDE ATTACKS

I've always held to the theory that the person I would most like to see on the other side of the negotiating table is a *friend* who is a *decision maker* who not only likes what I am proposing but who is *eager to help me* overcome the forces of resistance within his or her organization. This is the perfect customer: someone who not only buys into my proposal but also sells it to his or her company (often more enthusiastically than I do).

Unfortunately, the reality is that the world is largely made of imperfect customers.

This shouldn't surprise anyone. Customers are human. They don't behave admirably 100 percent of the time outside a negotiating session. Why expect them to be sterling characters at all times inside it?

But there are ways to negotiate within a hostile, imperfect world.

1. STAY IN THE MATCH.

Negotiating with an ornery customer is a lot like playing tennis with a powerful opponent. The key is to stay in the match. There's no clock, no time limit. As long as you don't lose match point, you have a chance to win. Your opponent may lose his or her stroke or concentration and may tire, while you gain your second wind. I've seen enough five-set matches where the winner lost the first two sets to know this is true.

The point is, in business you shouldn't self-destruct just because the other side takes a surprisingly aggressive attitude. Don't let personalities scare you away—because in a lifetime you are going to be selling to a lot of obnoxious people. Stay focused on your goals and stay in the game.

Years ago I dealt with a Marlboro cigarette executive in Switzerland. This man would say all the right things about being interested in our company and hiring us. Then he would set up meetings and not show up. When he did show up, he wouldn't do what he said he would do. In terms of our company, he was an absolute loser.

Now, the normal impulse is to run like hell away from such a customer—to save time and avoid frustration. (The message filters down through the company as "Forget the Marlboro man. He's a waste of time.")

But I was young and didn't realize what he was doing. I took a different tack. I pursued him all over Europe, trying to embarrass him into seeing me. I kept going back because he was making all these wonderful promises (and then backing off) and I believed him. It never worked. He never bought from me.

But my persistence eventually paid off. He later left Marlboro—and we were still in the game.

2. KEEP YOUR WALKAWAY NUMBER TO YOURSELF.

Every deal has a walkaway number, the absolute minimum terms you are willing to accept to complete a transaction.

27

Don't broadcast this number. In a hostile negotiation, if the other side knows the minimum you will accept, why should they pay any more?

Rather than reveal my absolute minimum, I find it much more effective in a back-and-forth sales situation to establish their *acceptable maximum*.

Most salespeople are afraid to deal directly with the question of how much money they are making. To me, an extremely good way of dealing with a customer who is squeezing you on price is to say, "Look, we have to make a profit. We don't want to make an unreasonable profit. But we have our overhead, our salaries, our bottom line, just like you. Here's what it costs us to make these widgets and here's the profit margin we need to make."

If you're being fair and accurate with people, they'll often surprise you—and pay you what you deserve.

3. IT ISN'T ALWAYS PRICE.

Price, it's commonly accepted, is the major source of contention in a negotiation. But it's rarely the reason a customer turns difficult and begins to attack.

How often have you and a customer agreed on a dollar figure and still the sale fell apart—because your timetables were at odds, because of who you assigned to the project, because a superior overruled the deal, or whatever?

A lot of times there's nothing you can do about this. It's just bad luck. But in my experience, when a customer becomes unreasonable in a sales situation, it's usually not because of price. It's price and one other reason.

In our business as sports marketing consultants to many corporations, we often find the biggest source of resistance to our proposals is the fact that we came up with the idea and the buyer didn't.

For example, let's say we come up with an idea for a sports event and approach a company to get involved in it. We offer to create the event. Produce it. Market it. Help the company maximize its benefits.

What we often find is that our proposal threatens the very person we're trying to sell it to. Perhaps he or she is ambitious and doesn't want to cede control to us. Perhaps he or she thinks that we'll come in as the sports experts and make him or her look bad by comparison or look redundant. Perhaps, under the "not invented here" syndrome, this person is worried that "this is a great idea, but I should have come up with it."

I don't know the reason for this resistance. But I do know that making the customer look good is often a more important component than price. And you don't find this out by automatically fighting back when a customer gets feisty. You learn it by just sitting back and hearing him or her out. The act of listening can be very persuasive.

4. BE HYPOTHETICAL.

As a general rule, the more specific the customer gets in his or her demands, the more hypothetical you should be. Thus, if they want to cut you down from $100,000 to $80,000, you can respond, "What if you still pay us the $100,000 but we'll throw in the following ingredients?" If you know your customers and can offer them new and valuable elements that cost you nothing, you will always get your asking price.

5. LOOK FOR DEAL MAKERS, NOT DEAL BREAKERS.

There's a school of thought that for every concession you make to a demanding customer, you should try to get something in return. I agree with that—to a point—but not if it forces the sales process into a time-consuming game of tit for tat. Eventually, one of you will come up with a reason to break the deal.

I rarely use the term *deal breaker* in a sales situation (unless I want the other party to walk away). I prefer *deal maker* because it forces the other party to commit.

When I make a major concession, I expect it to clinch the deal. I'm a big believer in the tactic of saying, "I'll do that, but that has to be the deal maker."

Thus, if I'm asking $95,000 for a project and you take a hard line, offering only $82,000 and insisting that I toss in several other ingredients, I might agree to those terms *if you unequivocally tell me we have a deal*.

The beauty of this tactic is its finality. It not only forces tough customers to make a commitment, but it stops them dead in their tracks from demanding more concessions.

NEVER TELL THEM WHAT YOU WOULDN'T DO

I was meeting with executives of a longtime customer of ours when the owner of the company turned to one of his trusted aides to ask how a particular negotiation was going.

The associate replied that the other side was making some tough demands, then added, "Of course, I told them they were out of their minds. We would never even consider those terms."

The owner cut him off and snapped, "Never tell them what you wouldn't do! The more options you have and the longer you can keep them, the stronger your position."

The owner made a valid point. In fact, it was so obvious you'd think he wouldn't have to remind his people about it. (It reminded me of the moment in *The Godfather* when the Don tells his hotheaded son, Sonny, "Never tell anyone outside the family what you're thinking.") But as I thought about it, it struck me that people in business abuse this rule all the time, perhaps without realizing it.

They say, "I'd never pay more than $100,000 for that"—when you know with a few sweeteners they'd pay a whole lot more.

They say, "I won't take less than $100,000 for that"—which is silly posing if you know they'd take less and downright irresponsible if you were willing to pay more.

They say, "I'll never work for that executive"—which needlessly cuts off a career option.

"Never tell them what you wouldn't do" is the flip side of an ultimatum. And we all know that ultimatums backfire as often as they work. Ultimatums can stop discussions dead in their tracks. They're potential deal breakers. They're like slamming the door shut in the other side's face and hoping the other side will knock on the door, pleading for you to let them in again. Quite often the knock never comes.

In my experience, when people abuse the "never tell them what you wouldn't do" rule, it's almost always out of weakness or because of misguided ego. The rule most often gets broken by people who exaggerate their value or the worth of their product or service. They take an overly aggressive position and close out more options than they create.

We had a client who was interested in writing a book. Fortunately, he was sufficiently celebrated that the international publishing community was interested in him too. The problem was his inflated sense of what his book was worth. His instructions to us were: "Don't come to me with any six-figure deals. I won't take an advance less than one million dollars." Who knows where he got that figure? Perhaps it was arbitrary. Perhaps that's what he heard one of his perceived rivals had received. Perhaps he simply liked the round simplicity of a million dollars. But there it was—a large number mocking and challenging us.

Quite often, an inflated dollar figure can be a tremendous spur to creativity. It's like setting "impossible" sales quotas; people come up with ingenious schemes to meet them. But this was not the case here. The best offers we could attract came to only half the amount. The client refused to consider the deal. No matter how unrealistic his expectations, he was backing down. What looked like a good deal to us just died on the table, and the only reason was ego.

It's ironic that people who tell the world what they won't do think they are demonstrating their confidence and strength. More often than not, they are merely proving their insecurity and weakness. Remember this the next time you hear yourself saying, "I won't take less than . . ." or "I won't pay more than . . ." Are you really prepared to close out your options? What may sound like bravado to you may actually be telling the other side something quite different.

LET'S HAVE BREAKFAST AT WIMBLEDON

Every once in a while you might find yourself in the uncomfortable position of having no options.

A client insists that he or she will work with only one executive at your company, even though several other executives might be more suitable or competent.

A large customer places such onerous conditions on doing business with him or her that your chances of success are almost nil.

Your boss green-lights an important project with one condition: You have to hire his or her nephew as a subcontractor.

How do you respond when your hands are tied or your back is up against the wall?

Some people fight. They accept the conditions and then do everything to demonstrate that they resent them. Eventually the transaction explodes in their face.

Some people flee. They refuse to work on anyone else's terms but their own—and consequently lose out on a lot of opportunities.

The most successful people neither fight nor flee. They accept the situation and find a way to twist it to their advantage.

Let me give you a sports marketing example from the not-so-distant past.

It might be hard to imagine a time when television did not exert a huge influence over sports events—especially today, when television can dictate everything from having all World Series games played at night to determining the starting time of the 100-meter dash at the Olympics so it airs at prime time in the United States.

But it was not so long ago that many sporting events tended to ignore the opportunities television offered.

Such was the case with our client Wimbledon.

Readers under age 30 might not remember that until the last decade, golf and tennis events in Great Britain never concluded on Sunday. Sunday was a traditional day of rest, a holiday with religious overtones. The final round of the British Open was played on Saturday. The men's final at Wimbledon was always played on Saturday.

As Wimbledon's marketing agents, assigned to broaden the tournament's global appeal and, among other things, sell broadcast rights to the championships in the United States, we would have been guilty of malpractice if we hadn't pointed out that this was a costly tradition.

We knew that there was a much larger potential audience of viewers on Sunday, when more people would be home. We had to persuade the Wimbledon committee to move the men's final to Sunday, which was not easy. On any sports governing body, there was always a cadre of "purists" who were suspicious of television, who would say, "Look, this is a sports event. Television is supposed to cover it as news. It is not supposed to control it."

Ultimately, a Sunday men's final happened because of money. NBC, the American network dealing with Wimbledon, offered x dollars for a Saturday championship and a multiple of x for a Sunday championship. Since all the money went to improving the state of British tennis, it wasn't long before Wimbledon—and, for that matter, all major events in the United Kingdom—concluded on Sunday.

I was proud of our company's role in all of this, how we had turned around some very conservative officials to our brand of common sense. We had sold an improved "product" to a major network for a better price and, in turn, helped raise money for British tennis. Our job was done.

But over at NBC their problems were just beginning.

Here they were, a major network making a "showcase" investment in time, resources, and cash in the most prestigious tennis tournament in the world—and the best time they could broadcast the men's final live from London was nine o'clock on Sunday morning on the East Coast, when most people are either asleep or getting dressed for church or reading the newspaper. Even demolition derbies and motorcross racing had better time slots!

I've always admired NBC's solution. In its own small way, it demonstrates how to react when your hands are tied.

NBC could have taped the championship and delayed showing it a few hours until Sunday afternoon. That's when they would draw the largest potential audience and maximize their advertising revenue. But that would have been a half-baked solution. The finals wouldn't have been live, and whatever NBC gained in audience and revenue would have been offset by the loss of drama. If you've ever watched a taped sports event, you know the slightly empty feeling you get knowing that you could turn on the radio or pick up the phone to learn who won. It would also have been a blow to NBC Sports' credibility. You can't call Wimbledon a showcase event and then delay showing it the way you would the usual Sunday filler.

A slightly better solution would have been to air the finals live, damn the early hour, and hope that tennis fans would gravitate to the broadcast. At least no one could accuse NBC of manufacturing suspense. Trouble is, NBC would not have been maximizing the situation or earning back their investment.

The most elegant solution, dreamed up by Don Ohlmeyer, the executive producer of NBC Sports, came in the form of three simple words: Breakfast at Wimbledon.

That's how NBC promoted the broadcast's unusual hour. In the finest if-you-have-a-lemon-make-lemonade tradition, NBC took the program's most obvious negative and turned it into a plus. In effect, NBC told the audience, "For one Sunday out of the year, do something different when you wake up. Stay home. Rustle up some breakfast. Invite friends over. Turn on the TV. Relax and watch something really special, something worth disrupting your usual routine for." The broadcast became an event.

NBC didn't fight. That is, they didn't whine or complain about a starting time that couldn't be changed.

Nor did they flee. That is, they didn't put on the championships and then bow out when the contract expired.

That happened a dozen years ago. NBC still calls the program *Breakfast at Wimbledon*, and the event becomes more popular every year.

What I most admire about NBC's solution, though, is its economy of effort. They didn't need to spend more money or mount an all-out media blitz to reorient people's thinking. All it took were three words that described the situation's most obvious aspect.

Keep that in mind the next time life tosses you an ornery challenge and your initial impulse is to fight or flee. More often than not, the answer is staring you in the face.

LEARNING TO LOVE LEVERAGE

Leverage is the secret weapon in any negotiation. But it is most valuable in getting delinquent customers to pay for what they bought. Dealing with deadbeats is never fun, but the problem is particularly acute in a personal services business. After all, if you sell someone a television set or a truckload of widgets and don't get paid, there's always a tangible asset that you can repossess.

You can't do that in a personal services business. Once you've given someone the benefit of your talent and time, you cannot get it back.

The first step to getting paid, of course, is to appreciate—no, *revere*—cash flow, that is, getting and using the money. It's how you stay and grow in business.

If you can do that, you're halfway there. Then all you have to do is apply some lessons in leverage.

LESSON 1. USE YOUR LEVERAGE EARLY ON.

The biggest mistake people make with leverage is waiting until it's too late to use it.

Customers who don't pay their bills usually leave a messy trail of clues behind them. Don't ignore them. If you hear from other suppliers that a customer is slow to pay, don't fool yourself into believing that you will be the one to change his or her habits.

If the customer has a questionable credit history, don't be timid about demanding as much money as possible up front. The customer should be eager to reestablish credibility—and meeting your terms up front is the only way to do that.

LESSON 2. MAKE SURE IT'S YOUR LEVERAGE.

There is leverage in almost any transaction. But that leverage is not always yours to use.

For example, we represent the international television rights of many major sports properties. We also represent the TV rights of a lot of smaller sports properties. As a result, we have to deal with dozens of foreign television networks, many of which (particularly beyond U.S., U.K., and European borders) are notoriously delinquent payers.

Consequently, it is not uncommon for us to have contracts with one network on six properties. Let's say the network has paid us for the broadcast rights to the National Football League, but has not paid us for five lesser properties. Ideally, we would love to tell this network, "You can't have the rights to the NFL next year until you pay up on everything else this year."

But we can't use that sort of leverage because it doesn't belong to us. It belongs to the NFL. It's not possible to clear our accounts with their markers.

LESSON 3. EMBARRASSMENT IS LEVERAGE TOO.

Sometimes the simple threat that you will tell the world about a customer's payment policies (or lack thereof) is more effective than all your invoices and legal notices combined.

A few years back one of our clients licensed his name to a computer game created by a new software company. The group was run by three professors at a major university who were moonlighting as entrepreneurs.

Ordinarily, this is the sort of situation where we would insist on most, if not all, of the client's fee up front. The company had no track record and no discernible revenues. The one thing they had going for them was their association with the university, which they were not shy about exploiting.

Our client took a third of his fee up front and was extremely cooperative in developing and promoting the product. He even made three separate speeches to the student body at the university.

Unfortunately, the computer group neglected to pay the rest of our client's fee. After nine months of listening to their excuses, the client used the only leverage he had. He wrote to the president of the university outlining the situation—that he had gone along with this venture because of the professors' affiliation with a prestigious institution, that he had spoken on campus three times for free, and that he felt he was being taken advantage of.

Before he mailed the letter, however, he showed it to the professors. In other words, he turned the tables on them. If they could leverage the university's name to get better terms from him, he could do the same.

A check for payment in full arrived the next day.

THE ART OF RENEGOTIATING

I always perk up when I read about a team-sport athlete who is unhappy about his long-term contract. You're probably familiar with the scenario: A superstar happily signs a contract to play ball for five years for a team for $20 million; that's an average annual salary of $4 million, which makes him one of the richest athletes in his game. Two years into the contract, the superstar looks around and sees that the upper limit of player salaries has shot up 50 percent. His peers (and some of his inferiors) are now signing long-term deals worth $6 to $7 million a year. The superstar is envious and hurt. He tells anyone who'll listen that he deserves better. He demands to renegotiate his contract.

What's wrong with this picture?

Leave aside the fact that $4 million is a lot of money to most people. (That's irrelevant when the going rate for your peers is $7 million.)

Leave aside the fact that most of us believe that a deal is a deal, that you learn to live with an agreement even when it tilts slightly in the other side's favor. If the superstar didn't like the original terms, he shouldn't have signed the contract.

Leave aside the fact that it's generally foolish to voice displeasure with a contract to the press and public. Taking a contract dispute public adds a whole new set of unwanted ingredients to the negotiation. Suddenly everything people do and say in what is essentially a very private matter (i.e., your paycheck) is open to public scrutiny. Quite often they negotiate with one eye on the contract terms and another eye on how it looks to their peers.

Leave aside all these considerations.

The real problem here is that the whole process of renegotiation has been handled so gracelessly. If there is an art to negotiation, there is also an art to *renegotiation*. The scenario above breaks all the rules.

RULE 1. RENEGOTIATE WHEN EVERYONE IS MOST HAPPY.

The best time to renegotiate or renew a contract is when both parties are most satisfied with the relationship. This could be one week after you sign the agreement or two years into a five-year term. There's no law that says you can't restructure a deal anytime, certainly not if both sides are eager to do it.

The sad truth, however, is that most people tend to renegotiate at the absolute worst time—when (a) they feel they are on the short end of the relationship or (b) the contract is about to expire and their bargaining position may not be at its peak.

Whenever we've done something exceptional for one of our clients, I urge that client's manager to discuss extending our representation agreement with the client, even if it still has a year or two to run. Why wait until the contract expires? The client is delighted with us; we're pleased to work for him or her. That's the best time to reconfirm and extend our relationship.

The same logic applies with a customer who has just heard some great news that may have nothing to do with your agreement. If a client company has just announced record profits or your contact at the company has just received a major promotion or bonus, that's a good time to talk to them about extending your agreement. Flush with success, they might be very accommodating.

RULE 2. BUILD RENEGOTIATION INTO THE CONTRACT.

People want to renegotiate because circumstances change. It's a lot easier to open a renegotiation if a contract recognizes those changing circumstances and mandates some revision in terms.

Patrick Ewing, the handsomely paid center of the New York Knicks, had a clause that let him out of his 10-year contract if at any point he was not one of the 4 highest-paid players in the NBA. This was the sports equivalent of an adjustable rate mortgage, with no downside risk to Ewing. If player salaries went up and Ewing fell out of the top four, he could force a renegotiation that might adjust his compensation. If salaries went down (which would defy all the laws of team sports!), it had no effect.

Whenever possible we try to insert similar "cost of living adjustments" into contracts. If a young athlete is happy getting a 10 percent royalty on the sale of apparel bearing his name, he might not be as happy 2 years later when he's an established superstar and apparel sales are going through the roof. That 10 percent royalty may seem paltry. Our contract should reflect that potential change in the athlete's status. We could mandate a renegotiation when apparel sales hit a certain figure. Or better yet, we can avoid renegotiation altogether by escalating the royalty rate as unit sales increase.

A contract that recognizes and rewards success is less likely to be disputed and more likely to last.

RULE 3. FIND ANOTHER INTERESTED PARTY.

It's a lot easier to force a renegotiation if you can insert the specter of other interested parties into the discussion. The other side does not want to get into a bidding war with new competitors for your product or services. Quite often the other side will be willing to renegotiate or extend an agreement midway through the term (even though there is nothing legally compelling them to do so) simply to shut those competitors out.

Some years ago we negotiated an exclusive recording contract with a major label for a young violinist in our classical music division. The financial terms weren't that impressive, but it was a five-year deal for two recordings a year. At the end of the contract, the violinist would have an impressive body of 10 recordings, which is an important asset in the development of a young classical artist.

As it turned out, the violinist's first three recordings were critical and commercial successes—so much so, in fact, that two other record labels were calling us with long-term offers that virtually let the artist dictate the terms. Ordinarily, this is like shooting fish in a barrel. When the time comes, you set up an auction and let the three labels bid up your client's price.

But for reasons of continuity and prestige, the artist was not interested in jumping to a new label. He was happy where he was.

Naturally, we didn't tell his record label that. But two years into the five-year deal, we did let the label know that other parties were making overtures. We suggested that maybe they would like to consider extending the agreement—with a better royalty rate for the artist, larger recording and promotion budgets, greater control for the artist over repertoire and choice of producers, and so on. With competing labels in the picture, it was relatively easy to extend the contract on our terms. And I don't think any of the label's executives felt that we were holding a knife to their throat.

Rule 4. Don't shoot fish in a barrel.

That record deal brings up an interesting point. Sometimes circumstances change so dramatically in your favor that you can call all the shots in a renegotiation. That's a tremendous advantage, but it's also a tremendous responsibility. Having the edge doesn't mean you always have to use it.

I remember in January 1960 Arnold Palmer agreed to play an exhibition in the fall in Elwood City, Pennsylvania, for a fee of $400 (decent money in those days). That was a great year for Arnold. In April he won his second Masters. That summer he won his first U.S. Open title. The week after the Open, a gentleman from Elwood City called me up and said, "That was a great win for Arnold. I guess you'll want to renegotiate his fee for the appearance at our club."

I must say I was tempted to take him up on his offer. People don't usually volunteer to raise a client's fee. But Arnold would have none of it.

"The fee stays," he said. "Those folks backed me long before I won the U.S. Open. The least I can do is return the favor." From then on Arnold made a point that Elwood City always paid less than the asking price for his time and services.

The line between the use of power and the abuse of power in a negotiation is a thin one. Sometimes there's more to be gained by holding back.

A NOTE TO MANAGERS: EVERYONE IS A NEGOTIATOR, EVERYTHING IS NEGOTIABLE

As someone who negotiates sales for a living, I've always been fascinated by the psychology of the people on the other side— the people who buy. Basically, buyers fall into two camps.

One camp of people insists on negotiating everything; to them, the list price is nothing but a point of reference, an absurd base figure that, through shrewdness, persistence, and sheer nerve, they intend to lower.

The second camp consists of people who never question the rate card. They always pay the quoted price. They are constitutionally incapable of negotiating. I'm not altogether sure why people think this way. I suspect some people are afraid of offending the seller, as if trying to negotiate is equivalent to accusing the seller of mispricing his or her product or service. Or perhaps they feel that negotiating is beneath them, that having to "nickel and dime" on price somehow downgrades them as a person. They don't want people to think they can't afford to pay the list price.

There's a paradox here. As a salesman, of course I'd much rather deal with the latter group. Dealing with people who think my pricing is fair makes my job much easier.

As an employer and manager of a company where millions of dollars of buying decisions are made every year, however, I prefer employees who fall into the first group. It frightens me to think that some of our people are paying full price for products and services that beg to be negotiated downward.

Over the years I've tried to make sure that our company's buying decisions are made by people who truly enjoy negotiating. And I urge our more timid types to emulate these fierce negotiators with some simple management principles.

1. MAKE AN ATTITUDE ADJUSTMENT.

Becoming a zealous negotiator first requires an attitude adjustment. You have to rethink your standards for what is and what isn't negotiable.

For example, it's ingrained in us to negotiate with certain people and not with others. You're supposed to negotiate with a used-car dealer or a merchant at a London flea market. Everyone knows that.

But you don't negotiate at a restaurant. If the menu says the filet mignon costs $27, you don't tell the waiter, "I'll give you $24." Everyone knows that too.

And yet, what if you were arranging a business dinner or wedding party for 32 people at that restaurant and wanted that same filet mignon as your entrée? Would you pay $27? Or would you say, "Look, since I'm guaranteeing you 32 meals, give me the filet mignon for $20." Most people wouldn't hesitate to negotiate on price. The simple fact that they are *buying in volume* reminds them that they have leverage and forces them to adjust their attitude about bargaining.

Every company has some form of leverage as a buyer of products and services. It could be the size of the order, or intimate knowledge of the seller's profit margins, or a willingness to pay immediately, or the promise of repeat business. It's in the company's interest to remind employees that these bargaining chips exist and should be used aggressively.

2. CREATE POLICIES THAT ENCOURAGE NEGOTIATING.

Some corporate policies can force people into bargaining for a better price.

For example, a few years ago we instituted a policy requiring three competitive bids on every purchase exceeding $500. We did this because we noticed that a lot of cozy relationships had developed between some of our employees and the vendors they regularly used. And that was hurting us on the bottom line, because no one at our company was challenging the vendors when they passed along their annual price increases.

Requiring competitive bids has changed that. But surprisingly, it has not done too much damage to our relations with our old vendors. We still do business with most of them—but at a price that's more to our liking than theirs.

3. TREAT GOOD BUYERS AS CORPORATE HEROES.

If a salesperson at a company closes a huge deal, word quickly spreads through the company. The salesperson is hailed as a hero and often awarded a bonus.

I think the same hero treatment should be given to employees who make great buys.

If an administrative staff employee negotiates a lease or service contract that reduces his or her company's operating costs by several hundred thousand dollars a year, that deal might have a more positive long-term effect on the bottom line than a onetime megasale. And yet that stellar negotiating effort often goes unnoticed and unheralded. Most companies don't send out memos hailing Jane Smith for the great lease she renegotiated. Buying is not perceived as glamorous or heroic. The honor of saving the company money rarely matches the glory of bringing it in.

If you recognize and honor people for negotiating great buys, your employees will not only learn from them but will take pride in emulating them.

4. ATTACK THE LITTLE DEALS AS WELL AS THE BIG ONES.

Not everyone is in a position to negotiate major purchases. But it takes just as much brains and initiative to negotiate the little deals.

I regularly review the administrative costs of our Manhattan facilities with our New York office manager. Her attitude is that no deal point is too small to question or fight for.

Whether we happen to be in an up or a down economy, she always takes the position that companies not only want our business, they need it. That makes them more willing to make concessions. And anything is fair game.

When she concluded that paying a personnel agency commission equal to 25 percent of a secretary's first-year salary was excessive, the agency eventually agreed to a flat fee for each employee we hire. Lesson: Flat fees are sometimes better than commissions.

When the cleaning company that maintains our three New York facilities balked at reducing their rates, she asked them to include our corporate apartment in the deal. They agreed. Lesson: For the same price you can get more service.

When our coffee supplier said it was impossible to switch to more efficient coffee-making machines, she talked to other vendors—at which point the coffee supplier miraculously found a way to accommodate her. Lesson: The "impossible" usually becomes possible when vendors hear you're shopping around.

When we added more copying machines to our office, she asked the vendor to reduce our per-copy price. Lesson: Increasing your volume is a license to renegotiate.

Taken individually, none of these "deals" will make or break the company. But take that attitude and multiply it by the dozens of vendors we deal with in each of our 69 offices and the economic effect is substantial.

Plus, if you can disseminate that attitude up and down your company, it will have a positive effect on how everyone operates, not only on how they negotiate purchases.

Most important, it doesn't cost the company anything to instill that attitude. As an investment, it is all reward and no risk.

WHAT YOU CAN LEARN FROM NEGOTIATING WITH YOUR SPOUSE

If I had to construct the ideal negotiating state, I often think it would be the negotiating relationship between a husband and wife. Considering all the mutual decisions a married couple has to make each day purely as a result of negotiating with each other, the spousal relationship may be the most efficient negotiating situation in the world. (I'm assuming that it's a relatively amicable, mature, functional union. A messy marriage on the brink of divorce is surely the least efficient negotiating situation.)

Whether they are negotiating little items such as who gets to shower first in the morning or major items such as where to go on vacation, couples maneuver and yield and assert themselves in fluid, effortless, and sometimes wordless ways. We can learn a lot about negotiating simply from analyzing the conditions that force them to behave that way. The following conditions make married couples better negotiators. Can you create the same conditions at work?

1. COUPLES HAVE TO SEE EACH OTHER AGAIN.

No matter how heated the debate, a couple knows they will have to face each other again when they turn in at night. That fact alone tempers how extreme and firm their positions are. When people know they will have to "do business" again with someone in the future, they tend to be more agreeable and less willing to pick a fight. Eliminating that sort of belligerence is good for any negotiation.

In the workplace, knowing you will have to deal with the other side again on other matters not only makes people more agreeable, it makes them less desperate. That's also good. People who are desperate to get a deal done tend to give up more than they should. Their desperation forces them into bad or mediocre deals.

My smoothest negotiations have always been with friends with whom I've done business for years and with whom I will continue doing business. Part of it, I'm sure, is our friendship. We know each other well; we know what we're looking for. Another part, I'm sure, is the fact that we know we'll meet again. If the deal doesn't make sense for either side, we can table it for another time or wait for the next idea. It's better to do nothing than to rush into a lopsided agreement. Knowing that we don't want that inequity hanging over our heads at the next meeting makes us smarter, more rational negotiators.

Injecting that sense of continuity into your negotiations may not ensure that you always get the best deal, but you're less likely to fall into a bad deal. The other side simply won't let it happen.

2. COUPLES RESPECT EACH OTHER'S TURF.

There are "no trespassing" zones in every marriage. It could be a touchy subject that automatically upsets the husband, an area of expertise peculiar to the wife, or an exclusive relationship that one partner has developed. Spouses have an instinctive feel for these areas. They know which lines they should not cross.

For example, I think I know more about tennis than the average person. My wife, however, is a professional tennis player. She's played on the Center Court of Wimbledon. I haven't. If we're playing doubles together and mapping out a strategy against the other side, I should naturally defer to her wisdom and experience. Whenever I forget this and suggest an alternative plan, she generally lets me know that the issue is nonnegotiable. Tennis is her turf. As a spouse, I'm sufficiently savvy not to argue the point.

It's tough to emulate that sort of sensitivity in a business negotiation. After all, you probably don't know the other side one-tenth as well as you know your spouse. But a little homework should tell you what the other side regards as inviolate turf.

For example, I've been negotiating endorsements and personal services contracts for athletes for 30 years. Athletes come in all shapes and sizes, with personalities to match. Some love contact with people; others are shy or simply antisocial. Whether they're nice or not, there's one contract point that they all regard as inviolate: *their time*.

To an active athlete, time is the most valuable commodity. It is finite and perishable. It is also a no-trespass zone. If our clients say they'll give the sponsor five days a year for making personal appearances and filming commercials, they

51

mean five days, not six days or five and a half. It's not because they're greedy or capricious or indifferent to the sponsor's needs. They simply know that *five* days is all they can spare. The more days they work for the sponsor, the fewer days they spend training, competing, and winning in their chosen sports, which is why the sponsor wants them in the first place.

You'd think that any sponsoring company with the slightest sensitivity to an athlete's schedule would appreciate that time is a no-trespass zone, a virtually nonnegotiable item. It's not as if we, as negotiators, are coy about it. We make our position clear from the beginning.

Yet after 30 years, I still find sponsors hammering away at the time issue in any personal services agreement.

They think that paying more will get them more of the client's time. (They're always amazed when they find out money is not the issue.)

They think that once they get the relationship going and get to know the athlete personally, they can chip away at his or her resolve during the year, squeezing more time commitments than the contract allows. (They're often surprised and personally hurt when we make them stick to the agreement.)

What's really amazing here is how counterproductive this is. Not only is the effort to move our client on the nonnegotiable issue of time commitment a waste of energy and goodwill, but it obscures all the issues where our client would be more yielding. The reality is, a negotiator who stayed out of the client's "time zone" would have a lot more freedom of movement in every other area, even on crucial issues such as money, renewal terms, and duration of contract.

As a general rule, if you can see which lines you cannot cross, you get a better view of which lines you can.

3. COUPLES REALLY NEED A MUTUAL BENEFIT.

A lot of businesspeople pay lip service to the "win-win" ideal in negotiating. But I don't know any skilled negotiator who isn't looking to win a little more than the other side. In business, you don't really need a mutual benefit to make a deal go through. It's nice when both sides walk away equally happy, but it's not absolutely necessary. Pushing for that edge is what makes a talented negotiator. It's also what kills a lot of deals.

It's different negotiating with a spouse. If either the husband or wife gets the better end of a negotiation, both of them might lose.

Let's say a couple is shopping for a new car. Before they negotiate with a car dealer, they have to negotiate with each other on the type of car they want. Let's say the wife wants a minivan to cart the children around in. The husband wants a large but sporty sedan that can double for business purposes. (If you think that's a sexist example, say the wife wants an import, the husband wants to buy American. The point is, they're far apart.)

If this were a negotiation at work—e.g., you and your boss discussing the company car you're entitled to—your car would be determined by some cold hard facts: What's the budget? What's available? Where's the best deal? Where does the company get group rates? You wouldn't negotiate about the car's make, color, and options because the boss wouldn't care.

It's not that simple in a marriage. Your car has to satisfy both of you. If the wife gets her way, the husband will always be grumbling. In fairly short order, the vehicle will become known as "her car." It won't be long before the husband finds a reason to buy "his car"—which may be more than the couple intended to spend on automobiles.

Smart couples avoid these irrational, infantile solutions. Since they really need a mutually beneficial outcome, they negotiate a compromise. They shop around. They go back and forth with each other. Perhaps they end up with a station wagon or a stylish sport utility vehicle that serves both family and professional purposes. Perhaps they acknowledge the stalemate and forgo the purchase altogether; their current car will do for another year or two. Either way, it's better than feuding, grumbling, or buying two cars when you need only one.

It's good to remember that dynamic in a business negotiation. If you and the other side are really interested in win-win, like a married couple you'll negotiate a deal that reflects that impulse or forgo it altogether. Either way, it'll be better than coming up with an agreement that leaves one or both of you unsatisfied and grumbling.

DON'T FORGET TO LOOK AT YOUR CARDS

Peter Lynch, the ultrasuccessful mutual fund manager and eminently quotable author, contends that there are a lot of mistakes that individual investors can make. But the most inexcusable is failing to do basic research on a company and plunging your money into a stock on a whim or the unsupported enthusiasm of a friend. "Many people," says Lynch, "invest in a way similar to playing poker all night without ever looking at their cards."

I think the same can be said of businesspeople in a negotiation. They don't know the full value of the hand they're holding because they forget to study their cards.

I can see how many of us fall into this trap. As sellers, we are constantly being encouraged to focus our attention on the buyers. We have to know what they need, what they can afford, what they have bought in the past, what they respond to, and what turns them off. With so much of our energy devoted to knowing the buyer, is it any wonder that some of us miscalculate the true strength of the cards in our own hand?

This mistake appears in many forms. Here are three preventive measures.

1. DON'T CATCH THE VIRUS OF DESPERATION.

Desperation is probably the most pernicious example. Sometimes external pressures—a boss looking over our shoulder, a quota, a deadline, a rival nipping at our heels—make us desperate to get a deal done. Unfortunately, I've never seen desperation improve anyone's negotiating position. It makes people too compliant and too willing to concede valuable deal points. Their negotiating objective is no longer *get the best deal* but rather *make sure the deal doesn't disappear.*

As a sales manager, I regard desperation as a killer virus that can wipe out a sales force. The moment one salesperson catches the fever and starts thinking that it's all right to shave a little here and there on deal points in order to close a sale, then everyone else thinks it's all right as well. That's why I'm constantly trying to inoculate our sales executives against the disease. At the same time that I'm exhorting them to sell, I'm also reminding them not to undersell our clients, that walking away from a bad deal is a laudable achievement too. I figure if they take a good look at our company's clients, properties, and track record, they'll have the same level of pride in what they're selling as I do. I can't ask for more than that.

Another reason people forget to look at their cards, of course, is because that is precisely what the other side wants them to do. Whenever the other side disparages your product, or gives you a "take it or leave it" ultimatum, or spends a lot of time on side issues, you can be sure they are trying to distract you, to take your eyes off your agenda and figure out theirs.

2. DON'T BE DISTRACTED BY A POT OF GOLD.

A rich customer is also another great distraction. Salespeople often forget themselves around a well-heeled customer, altering their behavior to please the prospect in ways they would never do around "ordinary" customers. It's not right, but it's human nature. People change when they see a pot of gold.

To stretch Lynch's poker analogy, it's not unlike playing against someone who has amassed a huge pile of chips. Some players become obsessed with getting some of those chips back. Instead of calmly assessing each hand they're dealt and betting accordingly, they get careless. They stop looking at their cards and focus instead on the other guy. Rather than fold with an obviously weak hand, they think their luck has to change or that the rich player's winning streak can't possibly continue. So they stay in the game longer than they should, throwing good money after bad.

In my younger days, I was sometimes guilty of this. I was overly impressed by wealthy corporations that had amassed huge piles of marketing chips. Whenever I heard that a company was making a large investment in sports, there was a part of me that thought our company should have a share of that business. Any entrepreneur worth his or her salt will recognize the feeling. If you hear that customers are on a buying spree, it's only natural for you to think they should be spending their money in your "store."

What's not natural, though, is unreasonably changing your business strategy or negotiating posture to please someone who has a big budget.

3. DON'T BE DAZZLED BY THEIR FINE CHINA.

There was a time in my career when I felt almost apologetic going hat in hand to corporations to convince them to spend some of their marketing budget on sports. The whole process was designed to intimidate a youngster like me. First, it would take me weeks or months to get through to the top decision maker. When I would finally call on the executive at his headquarters, the humility lessons intensified. My four-person office in Cleveland couldn't compare to the giant's edifice. His corridors were longer. His office was larger. His chairs were plusher. His mahogany conference table was shinier. His china service was finer. Even his secretaries were quieter.

And there I was, alone, clutching my briefcase, proposing that this busy executive should give a little more thought to the game of golf. For a while there, I was seriously dazzled by big organizations and didn't appreciate the true value of my "product line." I was looking at what I could get out of the customer rather than focusing on the unique things I had to offer.

Eventually I learned that big corporations are no more liberal with their money than small companies are. In fact, they're usually tighter. That's how they got to be big.

I also realized that big companies and well-heeled customers want you to be dazzled by their size and wealth. That's one of their major negotiating edges.

Most important, though, I learned that all companies, big or small, are made up of human beings who need to succeed and want to be liked—just like me. Why should I alter my sales pitch or discount my clients' value to accommodate them? If I thought my clients were the best in the world (which I did), how is that thinking changed by the wealth or lack thereof of a customer?

That insight, more than anything else, never lets me forget to look at my cards. If I like them enough to play them, I should play them for all they're worth.

● ● ●
THE McCORMACK RULES

- There's a difference between being liked by the other side and needing to be liked. Needing to be liked is a weakness, especially if satisfying that need compels you to sacrifice negotiating points.

- Many people can't cope when the discussion takes a 90-degree turn or the issues on the table veer out of bounds. They're so locked into their position, they don't realize that circumstances can change in the middle of a negotiation and render all previous agreements moot. A talented negotiator knows how to scramble and improvise.

- Integrity in a negotiator is like consistency in an athlete. It's not apparent right away. It takes time for other people to appreciate it.

- The smartest person in the room is not necessarily the best negotiator. In fact, the smartest people may be the worst negotiators, especially if they think they have all the answers and, consequently, neglect to ask the right questions.

- The best negotiator regards everything as negotiable.

- Patience may be a virtue, but in negotiating it is a weapon. If you can outwait the other side, you can usually outnegotiate them.

- If you have nothing else going for you but a superior ability to communicate, you can be a superior negotiator.

- Quite often the most persuasive negotiator in the room is the one who has the greatest expertise and mastery of the details.

- If every negotiation consists of major and minor negotiating points, the biggest irony is that it's usually the minor issues that can kill the deal.

- Customers are human. They don't behave admirably 100 percent of the time outside a negotiating session. Why expect them to be sterling characters at all times inside it?

- Negotiating with a really difficult customer is a lot like playing tennis with a powerful opponent. The key is to stay in the match. As long as you don't lose match point, you have a chance to win.

- Every deal has a walkaway number, the absolute minimum terms you are willing to accept to complete a transaction. Don't broadcast this number. In a hostile negotiation, if those on the other side know the minimum you will accept, why should they pay any more?

- Price may be the major source of contention in a negotiation. But it's rarely the reason a customer turns difficult. It's price and something else.

- The more specific the customer gets in his or her demands, the more hypothetical you should be.

- Never tell them what you wouldn't do! The more options you have and the longer you can keep them, the stronger your position.

- The biggest mistake people make with leverage is waiting until it's too late to use it.

- The best time to renegotiate or renew a contract is when both parties are most satisfied with the relationship.

- If a salesperson at a company negotiates a great sale, the salesperson is hailed as a hero. The same hero treatment should be given to employees who negotiate great buys.

- When people know they will have to "do business" again with someone in the future, they tend to be more agreeable and less willing to pick a fight.

- Having the edge doesn't mean you always have to use it.

- It takes just as much brains and initiative to negotiate the little deals.

CHAPTER 3

The Tools at Their Disposal

WHAT PATTERN IS THE OTHER SIDE WEAVING?

One of the best negotiators I've dealt with was a limousine driver in California. I had hired the car and driver to take me and my secretary from Palm Springs to the Peninsula Hotel in Beverly Hills, a relatively simple two-and-a-half-hour drive during which I hoped to plow through a large pile of correspondence. (That's the best justification for the expense of a limousine: You get a tranquil environment that lets you work when most people are wasting away behind a wheel staring at road signs. You also get an allegedly professional driver who knows where he or she is going, even if you don't.)

Somewhere near Los Angeles, the trip went awry. Low on gas, the driver turned off the freeway to find a gas station. This side trip took 25 minutes as the driver stopped several times to get directions, only to end up in one of the more desolate, burned-out sections of East Los Angeles. Visions of Tom Wolfe's *Bonfire of the Vanities* came to mind, but I was soon distracted by our driver's total inability to relocate the freeway. Another 20 minutes passed as we toured some of the more infamous streets of South-Central Los Angeles.

Any work I had intended to do was interrupted by my growing irritation with the driver. When we finally arrived at the hotel, an hour late, I let him know precisely what I thought of his incompetence and what I intended to tell his boss, none of which would be flattering. I also intended to challenge the bill.

At the end of my tirade, the driver said, "Go easy on me. I've got seven kids at home."

With that simple appeal for mercy, the driver completely wiped out both my personal animus toward him and my negotiating posture with the limousine company. How could I not be sympathetic to someone supporting a large family? Was I really willing to put his livelihood at risk by complaining to his superiors? The funny thing is, this play for sympathy worked. As far as I'm concerned, the bad trip is forgotten . . . except for one nagging thought: I wonder how many other trips this driver has messed up and how many other times he's told a client about his seven kids. Is it a onetime occurrence or is it his negotiating style? Unless I meet him again, I'll never know.

It's different in business. If you regularly deal with certain people, at some point, if only through frequency and repetition, you have to pick up some insights about their negotiating styles. People have habits, tendencies, and tics. See enough of them and you can detect a pattern to their negotiations. Here are four patterns that you ignore at your peril.

1. THE POOR-MOUTH PATTERN

I've been doing business with a friend for over 20 years who opens every contract renewal by (a) telling me what a lousy year he's had and (b) enumerating all the areas where he feels our company has dropped the ball on his behalf. That's his technique: He poor-mouths his bank account and our performance. It's so obvious that I even joke about it now *before* he launches into his spiel. The fact that he's still a friend and still a customer after two decades should tell you something about the value of recognizing a negotiating pattern. If you see it, you can deal with it.

2. THE CONCESSION PATTERN

Everyone, consciously or not, has a pattern for conceding points in a negotiation.

Some people stair-step their concessions: They give away points in increasingly larger increments, starting out small and holding back on the big concession they hope you never ask for. (This is a smart strategy.)

Other people reverse the pattern, shrinking their concessions as the process drags on. (This is a good way to speed up a negotiation.)

Still other people make concessions and then waste time trying to win them back. (This can be maddening.)

There's no single ideal concession pattern. But it's a sin not to be aware of it—in yourself as well as others.

3. THE ACCESSION PATTERN

This is an interesting flip-flop on the stair-stepped concession. Instead of conceding points, you acquire them.

I noticed this pattern some years ago with a fellow I had always enjoyed dealing with. One reason I enjoyed him was his seemingly nonsense-free approach to deal making. He didn't haggle over price. If I quoted a figure, he accepted it on the spot. He could afford this, I learned, because as we went along he would keep adding costly features—for free!—to the deal. If the term of the deal I quoted on was two years, he'd blithely bump it up to three years. If the agreed territory was, say, North America, he'd assume it was the world. Quite often, because he was paying top dollar, I would let him get away with it.

Once I caught on, this accession pattern fascinated me, largely because it was so blatant. It was as if you walked into an auto showroom, asked about a car listed at $20,000, and accepted the salesperson's opening quote of the list price.

After the two of you shake hands, you slyly add, "That includes leather seats, of course?

"And antilock brakes?

"And dual airbags?

"And an extended warranty?"

And the salesperson agrees to everything—because you're paying the list price. Instead of negotiating $3,000 off the $20,000 price tag (which is what most people try to do), you've grabbed onto $4,000 worth of free features. You've paid $20,000 for a $24,000 car.

Look out for this pattern when people agree to the first quote out of your mouth. Be particularly alert to their follow-up requests and assumptions. They may be grabbing more than you think you are giving.

4. Splitting the difference

You'd think this would be the easiest pattern to spot. It's how most of the world "negotiates." You want $20. I offer $10. We settle on $15. And quite often we both end up not entirely happy. That's the problem with splitting the difference. It's so common and so easy to do that most people aren't aware they're doing it.

On the other hand, some people *live* to split the difference. Their first offers are intentionally so extreme—high if they're selling, low if they're buying—that splitting the difference is an excellent and desirable result for them.

This tactic is even more dangerous when it is employed constantly, when it is the dominant pattern of a negotiation. If people on the other side are strategically exaggerating their position on *every* point, waiting for you to split the difference, they will whip you every time.

BLOCK THAT TACTIC!

Most of us go into a negotiation with a good idea of what we want, what we're going to say, and what is not worth mentioning. If we have prepared well, we probably have a good idea of what the other side is going to say as well—and have an answer ready for every question they throw at us. If we're lucky, we can transform the negotiating process into a pleasant dialogue that moves forward rationally and logically to a mutually desired conclusion.

Unfortunately, the other side doesn't always follow our script.

If we are selling, they may not share our high opinion of our product or service. They may have policies against completing the sale. They may not have the money. They may not have the staff to implement the sale, no matter how artfully we conclude the negotiation.

All of these can be legitimate stumbling blocks in a sales negotiation.

But after years of negotiating, I've noticed that the same stumbling blocks keep appearing over and over again. In fact, certain arguments come up with such numbing regularity that I no longer regard them as arguments. I see them for what they really are. They are tactics, little maneuvers designed to weaken my position but not to the point where I walk away from the table. They are not accurate indicators of what the other side thinks of me or my position. They are simply intended to elicit a response.

In that sense, negotiating tactics are like moves in a chess game. You don't overreact or get angry when someone makes a daring move in chess. At a certain level of play, you're expected to be familiar with the move, and you're expected to stay at the table and respond.

The same thing happens in negotiations. At a certain level, you should be recognizing the other side's tactics and be sufficiently skilled to respond in kind.

Here is some advice on how to deal with tactics from the other side of the negotiating table.

1. Don't accept the negative attack.

Some people are bullies. You walk into their office and they pummel you with disparaging remarks about your company or your product.

This is the crudest negotiating tactic of all. But some people have elevated it to an art form. They can turn the brutal invective on and off like a water faucet.

I know one executive who's probably not even aware he does it. Whenever I meet with him to discuss a new project, he feels compelled to bring up a past project and hone in on the one or two details out of 100 that we accomplished less than perfectly. His tirades are so predictable they are almost comically easy to counter. For years now, the moment I greet him I make a point of bringing up our alleged errors first. I literally disarm him by taking away his one and only weapon.

Incredibly, some people—particularly young or inexperienced negotiators—fall for this tactic.

Perhaps they are intimidated by the assault. (That's what the attacker wants. It's better to not react at all.)

Perhaps they feel guilty or responsible. (This is rarely true. Remember, a bully doesn't need a valid reason to attack; it's in his or her nature to pick on someone who won't fight back.)

Perhaps they believe that anyone venting that much fury must have a legitimate gripe. (Again, the attack is a tactic designed to break down your position. It's not personal. It's not heartfelt. It probably isn't true. Ask yourself: If this individual is so mad at us, why are we still talking? Why do we continue doing business together?)

2. DON'T ACCEPT THEIR ULTIMATUM.

When people want to suggest that they are prepared to back out of a negotiation, they usually turn to a familiar set of phrases, such as "That's all I can afford" or "You have to do better than that" or "Take it or leave it."

I can see why. These phrases work. They sound like ultimatums. They can scare the uninitiated negotiator into conceding anything in order to keep the buyer at the table and save the deal.

But in reality, they are tactics. They are not genuine (if they were, you would have to back down or walk away). They are a test, another chess move to prod you into action, to test out your counterpunch.

In my experience, ultimatums are rarely the end of a negotiation. They are the beginning.

3. DON'T GIVE THEM AN EASY OUT.

The buyer's easiest out from any negotiation is this: "I love your concept. I want to do it. But I don't have the budget."

Oddly enough, this is not a tactic. When buyers tell you this, they really mean it. They usually don't have the budget!

But it's worth mentioning in a discussion on tactics because it is also an opportunity for you to ease into a negotiation at a price the buyer can't refuse.

For example, in our business of selling sponsorships to sports events, we're frequently told, "I don't have the budget." That's not surprising. Sports sponsorship is a fairly untraditional media buy, and the price of entry is high.

But after months of identifying, pursuing, and wooing a prospect who admits to loving our concept, we'd be fools to let the prospect leave the table.

Sometimes we work for nothing. We literally give the property away and let the customer pay us whatever he or she thinks it's worth after the fact.

Sometimes we defer payment. This is sort of like buying a car and paying for it later. But in our case it's much better. Our people rub shoulders with the customer's people for a year. They see how we operate. We become friends. If we do our job well, they'll not only pay us what they owe, but they'll go out of their way to find the budget for us in year two and beyond.

When people tell you their budget is zero, your best response is, "I can work with that."

4. BEWARE THE BULK ORDER.

Buyers are always looking for volume discounts—without actually buying the designated volume. If they secretly want 1,000 units of your product, they'll try to get you to quote a price for 10,000 units or 50,000—and then start negotiating at the lower unit price.

That's a fairly transparent tactic, requiring nothing more from you than the resolve to stick to your rate card.

But a clever negotiator can lure you into a discount in much more subtle ways.

Real estate developers, for example, are masters at winning concessions from contractors by holding out the promise that there will be more work on other projects.

We've run into customers who insist on removing certain features from our proposal in order to lower the price, and then, having secured that price, try to negotiate those features back.

Some customers like to offer technical support—usually in the form of personnel—to lower the price, and then they never deliver their people.

There's some good news here, though. After all, when someone asks, "What if I buy two," if you are patient and disciplined you can double the sale.

5. DON'T FALL FOR THE GOOD COP.

The "good cop/bad cop" tactic is one of the most familiar routines in negotiation. We've all seen it. Two people show up at the negotiating table. One of them is the designated bad guy whose job is to chew you up, wear you down, make outrageous demands, and challenge you every step of the way. The second person is the good guy, usually a senior person whose job is to apologize for his colleague's bad manners. Of course, you gravitate toward the good guy—because his temperament, demeanor, and negotiating position appear to be more inviting.

The funny thing about the good cop/bad cop tactic is that I am very good at detecting it—but I fall for it anyway!

In my heart I want to believe the good cop is on my side, even when my brain is telling me he or she is playing a role—one that's not necessarily in my best interest. (I suppose this is a reflex from childhood: When we don't get our way with one parent, we instinctively turn to the other. What we don't realize, of course, is that parents have a tacit agreement never to contradict each other in front of us.)

How do you overcome this tactic? Simple. Shut out the good guy. Focus all your energies on turning the bad guy around to your point of view. If you can't do that, you haven't lost anything—because you won't do any better with his partner.

LET THE OTHER SIDE SHOW YOU HOW IT'S DONE

People have a natural tendency to want to show the other side in a negotiation how smart they are, how well they know their business. But there will always be times when the other side is smarter than you. You can let this intimidate you. You can deny it and fight a losing battle. Or you can admit it—and let the other side teach you a thing or two.

I've always thought that Bjorn Borg's most lasting achievement was not his five consecutive Wimbledon titles, but rather that he single-handedly elevated the game of an entire generation of tennis players. Borg hit the ball with such overpowering topspin, his opponents had to enhance their repertoire simply to stay on the court with him. Those recalcitrant players who insisted on playing their own unchanging game against Borg soon fell off the tour. The smart ones, who were willing to adapt and learn from Borg and challenge him with some topspin of their own, ultimately improved their game—and on occasion beat him.

I noticed the same sort of effect in one of our company's first forays into television. MCA, the giant media conglomerate that owns Universal Pictures, wanted to produce a series of televised "golf challenges" using our clients. At the time, we were novices in television. We didn't know what a program cost or how it was produced. We didn't know how to write a contract or what points to demand on behalf of our clients.

Our counterparts at MCA, of course, were experts at this, and quite frankly, we were a little intimidated by them. If MCA was Borg, then we were a weekend hacker. They had years of experience in dealing with stars, budgets, production schedules, and contracts. We didn't.

But at some point we realized that dealing with such a formidable opponent could actually be to our advantage—if we were willing to acknowledge the opponent's strength.

Since we trusted MCA, why not let them draft the contract? With years of trial and error behind them, their boilerplate was probably better than our best effort. They knew the key points. They knew the troublesome clauses. They might highlight or concede points that we would never have considered.

By keeping an open mind, we basically let MCA show us how to write a state-of-the-art television contract—one that has served as our model for three decades.

WHEN YOU HEAR ONLY WHAT YOU WANT TO HEAR

The trouble with numbers is that we are more inclined to trust them than doubt them—even though most of us know that numbers can be manipulated to say whatever we want them to say.

The numbers that most worry me in a negotiation are the ones that sound too good to be true—because they delude me into hearing what I think I want to hear rather than the truth.

A company once approached us with a potentially lucrative merchandising concept for one of our clients. If everything went according to plan, the client stood to earn $400,000 a year for doing virtually nothing. If the client received the money, fine. But the approach and the dollar figure were based on very heady assumptions. It was the absolute best-case scenario.

A closer reading of the agreement showed that our client was guaranteed only $25,000 a year. That reflected the worst-case scenario.

But human nature being what it is, people are rarely inclined to describe their efforts in worst-case terms. And so that transaction began to take on a life of its own within the company. It became "big."

Over time the $400,000 figure was bandied about so loosely and repeated so often that it became a fixed number. Worse yet, it created a ripple effect. The number colored other agreements. Our people started to alter or delay other projects for fear they would negatively affect the "big" $400,000 deal.

Whenever I hear people in our company describe a stunning negotiation, I ask myself: Are we hearing only what we want to hear? Is the other side describing this in similar terms?

In this particular case, I doubt if the head of the merchandising company was sitting across town boasting, "We came up with a concept where McCormack's client earns $400,000 a year for doing nothing." He was more likely saying, "Hey, we got their client for $25,000. What do you think of that?"

ARE PEOPLE PLAYING WITH YOUR REACTION TIME?

I used to sit on the board of directors of a well-run company. The board would gather at least twice a year at company headquarters to review how things were going. The meetings were fascinating, not so much because of what was discussed but because of how the chairman and CEO controlled the meeting. He was a very thorough and precise individual who paid attention to the smallest detail. He knew exactly how much time he wanted to spend on each subject on the agenda, and the meetings never fell behind schedule.

To the untrained eye, observing this hyperefficient CEO as he sat at one end of the conference table, there was no question that he was in control of the meeting.

At the other end of the table, however, sat the chairman emeritus, a courtly man well into his seventies who had built the company, who had handpicked this CEO as his successor, and who remained the company's largest shareholder. Although he was extremely reserved at these meetings and gave the CEO tremendous latitude, there was no doubt among any of us in the room that this elder statesman remained the real center of power at the company.

I always admired how the CEO handled this situation—how he asserted himself at the board meetings and yet always appeared to be deferring to the chairman emeritus. But my admiration grew immeasurably at one meeting when I noticed a little maneuver the CEO used to hand out reports.

If he had 12 areas of company business to discuss, he would prepare 12 separate reports—one on each area—and hold off distributing these reports until we reached that part of the day's agenda. His assistant, who also took the minutes of the meeting, would pick up a stack of reports and walk around the table distributing a copy to each of us.

I happened to be sitting next to the chairman emeritus on one particular day, and I couldn't help noticing that each time the assistant came to me, I would receive a photocopy of the report—and the chairman emeritus would get the original! (Note: This was some time ago, before document processors and laser printers made everything look like an original.)

This minor, barely perceptible tactic was a masterstroke of common sense. True, the CEO was stroking the old man's ego, but his method was so subtle that you couldn't do anything but admire it. In effect, he was using a mere document a dozen times in one meeting to show his deference to the chairman emeritus. And none of the directors was aware of it. It was like a private conversation between the two men, as if the CEO was whispering to the older man, "You're still the boss."

I have to believe that understanding of people and power (and presumably there were other acts of deference that I was not aware of) is what gave the CEO the license to run the meetings and the company in such a strong, confident manner.

Later on, as I thought about the CEO's gamesmanship with the reports, I realized that he was executing a larger strategic point, again very subtle but a little more insidious. Not only was he using the reports to play with the chairman emeritus's ego, but he was also playing with our reaction time. By handing out the reports piecemeal and only as we were about to discuss the subject they addressed, he was basically controlling how much time we had to study the reports, analyze the numbers, read between the lines, compare notes among ourselves, and come back at him with tough questions if we had any. He was cancelling out our power to criticize him on the spot.

Again, it was a masterstroke of common sense and power politics. By delaying the distribution of the reports, he had tilted the field of debate in his favor.

Ideally, all of the directors should have received the reports days or weeks before the meeting so we would have time to react intelligently and fashion informed questions.

I realize now that this manipulation of people's reaction time goes on at all levels of business.

Someone once told me that Pauline Kael, the legendary film critic for *The New Yorker*, was notorious for filing her weekly reviews at the last possible moment. It was not because she was dilatory or inefficient. She simply didn't want some editor changing her copy. Pushing her deadline to the limit meant her editors had less time to toy with her words. She played with their reaction time by reducing it.

If people devote this much care to manipulating the reaction time of others in board meetings and with writing assignments, you can be sure they're doing the same in a negotiation, where gaining or losing time to think is a vital issue.

At its most blatant level, when the other side gives you a verbal deadline ("We need your decision now!"), they are reducing your reaction time.

Likewise when they delay sending you the contract until the last possible moment.

On the other hand, when the other side claims they have to consult with an absent decision maker ("I'll get back to you after I check with my boss"), they are trying to increase their reaction time.

Likewise when they claim they don't have the backup material you requested.

Or when they adjourn the meeting for the day after you've presented your position but before they've presented theirs.

Or when they bring technical experts into the meeting to digress on obscure points while the real decision makers consider their options.

Or when they plead ignorance ("We need to study this issue").

These are all effective tactics used to guarantee that their reaction time is greater than yours.

I mention these tactics not to admire or endorse them but more in the way of a warning. When people try to manipulate your ability to react properly to something, they often have something to hide. If people are playing with your reaction time, that should be your signal to react with more care than ever.

● ● ●
THE McCORMACK RULES

- If you regularly deal with certain people, at some point, if only through frequency and repetition, you have to pick up some insights about their negotiating styles.

- Some people *live* to split the difference. Their first offers are intentionally so extreme that splitting the difference is an excellent and desirable result for them.

- When someone tells you that his or her budget is zero, your best response is, "I can work with that."

- You have three options when the other side is smarter than you. You can be intimidated. You can deny it. Or you can admit it—and let the other side teach you everything they know.

- The numbers that should worry you most in a negotiation are the ones that sound too good to be true.

CHAPTER 4

Question Everything

LEARN TO ASK, "SAYS WHO?"

A friend suggested the title for this book should be *The Art of the Negotiation*—with the emphasis on "*the* negotiation," because no two negotiations are the same. What you applied two weeks ago won't work again. In fact, if you have a discernible technique or pattern, it can work against you at times.

I agree with that. Each negotiation is different, and therefore demands that you question and rethink your approach. Negotiating is not a technique that you can plug into any situation and play out. You have to begin each negotiation anew, with a clean slate. And you have to treat your tried-and-true tactics with extreme skepticism.

But I would take it a step further. You have to apply that same skepticism to the other side. You have to question their approach and treat each of their assumptions and statements with extreme skepticism. I feel so strongly about this that I daresay it's the cornerstone of my negotiating style. When I listen to the other side outline their position, I'm always thinking to myself, "Says who?"

If they tell me their price is x, my instinct is not only to wonder how I can reduce it to one-half x (that's what negotiating is all about) but to question how they got to x.

If they tell me they'd like our client at the meeting, I want to know why.

If they're giving me a negotiating deadline, I want to know what's the rush.

If they're offering a suspiciously high price, I want proof of their ability to pay. I also want to know why they're paying so much.

A big part of this, of course, is that I'm inherently suspicious. I wasn't always this way. But when you make your living representing celebrated athletes, you inevitably run into people who want to sidle up next to those athletes—and their motives aren't always pure or altruistic. Quite early in my learning curve as a negotiator, I became suspicious as a shield for my clients. You only have to go through one or two deals in which the other side turns out to be playing by their own private set of rules before you learn, as a matter of policy, to question the rules.

When I was starting out in Cleveland in the early 1960s, we would often get letters or phone calls offering one of our top golfers a ludicrously large amount of money to headline a series of exhibitions in the Far East. Now, the normal impulse with such a generous offer would be to congratulate yourself on being in the right place at the right time with the right product and say, "Where do I sign?" But I gradually learned to treat extreme financial offers with extreme suspicion. Bogus offers turned out to be one of the occupational hazards of our business. A would-be sports promoter would float a big number to get our superstar's commitment and then use that commitment to line up the financing and the rest of the field. In the meantime, our client had locked that time period into his schedule with no guarantee that the event would come off as planned or that he or she would be paid the sum that proved so attractive in the first place.

As a matter of course, we learned to treat big offers as red flags, not golden eggs. We questioned everything. We asked for references, letters of credits, and all sorts of guarantees before we let our superstar commit.

I'm convinced that some form of "Says who?" skepticism, applied vigorously with strangers and reasonably with friends, can improve your position in any negotiation.

It's a matter of attitude. I look at every major deal point proposed by the other side as a unilateral decision that has been made without me. It's my job as a negotiator to take umbrage at unilateral decisions that shut me out.

Adopting that attitude should not be a huge mental leap. If your parents unilaterally decided whom you should marry, you would automatically be outraged at their presumption. The decision is so out of line with Western custom and privileges that you would be within your rights to treat the matter as a joke.

For a less outrageous example, what would you do if your parents unilaterally decided what college you should attend? You probably wouldn't hesitate to challenge them and tell them they were out of line (even as you acknowledged that they were footing the bill and, therefore, should have some say in the matter). Before you asked how they came up with their choice, before you demanded to have a majority voice in the decision, I would think you'd want to know who and what gave them the right to make that decision. You would and should be outraged at their presumption and impertinence.

It's really no different in a business negotiation. Every time you let the other side go unchallenged in quoting a price, setting a deadline, dictating a procedure, or determining who says yes or no, you are letting the other side make a unilateral decision. You are letting the other side write the rules of the negotiation (rules that surely won't be written to your advantage). In effect, you are excusing their presumption and impertinence.

You can do worse than look at each negotiation as an exercise in presumption (the other side's), differing only in the degree of presumption. In some negotiations, the other side decides whom you should marry. In others, they decide what college you should attend. Either way, you should be prepared to be outraged. That attitude will rarely cost you. More likely, it will catch the other side by surprise.

I remember seven years ago when our client Herschel Walker, the great running back for the Dallas Cowboys, was traded in midseason to the Minnesota Vikings. Connoisseurs of NFL personnel decisions regard the deal as one of the most significant (and ultimately one-sided) trades in league history. In Walker the Vikings acquired a proven runner who could spark their offense and lead them immediately to the Super Bowl. The Cowboys, on the other hand, were looking toward the future. They had lost 15 of their 16 games the year before with veteran players and desperately needed fresh young talent. So they did what any mature business looking to change direction would do: They sold assets. In Walker, the Cowboys had a valuable asset the Vikings needed. So the Cowboys' owner, Jerry Jones, dealt Walker to the Vikings for five players as well as Minnesota's first-round and second-round draft picks for the next three years. In effect, Minnesota was mortgaging its future for the immediate payoff Walker represented. Dallas was losing a star player to increase its access to the college talent pool for the next three years.

(In hindsight, it was a brilliant deal for Dallas and a disaster for Minnesota. Walker never fit into the Vikings' offensive scheme and was traded to another team two years later. Dallas went on to win two Super Bowls with all its top draft choices. But that's another story.)

What sticks out in my mind is Walker calling his agent, Peter Johnson, the head of our team sports division in Cleveland, the day of the trade. The conversation went like this:

Walker: Peter, I've been traded to the Vikings.
Johnson: What do you think about that?
Walker: I don't really want to go.
Johnson: Well, don't do anything yet.

The more Johnson mulled over this news, the more outrageous it seemed. Walker had been extremely happy in Dallas. He had led the league in rushing the year before. He was popular with the fans. He had lucrative endorsement contracts with local merchants and was getting involved with the community's cultural and civic affairs. (At one point, he danced in leotards onstage with the Fort Worth Ballet, which generated unprecedented national publicity for the company.) Yet here were the Cowboys and Vikings making a unilateral decision about Walker that would directly affect his professional and financial circumstances for years to come—without letting him in on the decision! They were treating him like chattel.

This sort of thing had been going on for years. Players were traded at a moment's notice based on management's whim. In no other field could an organization send an employee to a competitive company without the employee having a say in the matter. But professional sports in the United States was unique. Management wrote the rules, and no one was in a position to question the rules. (Over time, a few top players fought this inequity by insisting on no-trade clauses in their contracts; they couldn't be traded without their approval. But Walker at the time did not have a no-trade clause.)

Johnson opted to challenge the rules. He knew there was nothing he could do to keep Herschel Walker in Dallas, but he could try to make Dallas pay for sending him away.

Within an hour of hearing the news, he called Cowboys owner Jerry Jones and said, "Jerry, you're getting what you want out of this deal. Minnesota is getting what it wants. But by leaving Dallas, my client Herschel Walker will lose marketing opportunities. I'm calling to tell you that Herschel will not report to the Minnesota Vikings unless you compensate him for moving. We want $1.25 million payable in one lump sum by tomorrow or the trade won't happen."

To Johnson's amazement, Jones agreed and the money was wired to our Cleveland office the next day.

In hindsight, it's easy to say that Johnson shouldn't have been amazed. Johnson had some crucial leverage on his side. Walker had managed his money well. He was financially independent. He didn't need to play football for a living. There were plenty of other things he could do, and both Dallas and Minnesota knew it.

But I'm convinced that Johnson's greatest leverage (and real achievement) was his willingness to question the rules by which Dallas and Minnesota were playing. NFL owners had been trading players among themselves with impunity for seven decades. The system suited them fine. Why shouldn't it? They wrote the rules. Until the Herschel Walker trade, no player had ever challenged the owners and said, "I see what you get out of this trade, but what's in it for me?"

That's the beauty of questioning the rules. Once you see every feature of the other side's negotiating position as a unilateral decision made without your input, you begin to look for ways to inject yourself into the decision. But you cannot inject yourself until you appreciate how ruthlessly or shrewdly the other side has kept you out.

THE MYTH OF THE NEGOTIATING TABLE

I am puzzled when I hear businesspeople refer to the "negotiating table." Things will improve if they can just get the other side to "sit down at the table." They second-guess others because they "left money on the table."

I don't know about you, but my successful negotiations have rarely been conducted sitting around a table. More likely, the nuts and bolts of hammering out agreeable terms have been handled on the telephone, or over the course of a friendly meal in a restaurant, or by exchanging letters or faxes, or by middlemen (agents, brokers, attorneys, etc.) employing phones, meals, letters, and faxes.

As far as I can tell, only diplomats and labor leaders like to conduct their deal making around a table. I'm not sure if they gather around a table to settle their wars and labor disputes as a public relations stunt (so they can be seen actually doing something). But the futility of most of these negotiations—they rarely satisfy both sides and they take weeks, months, sometimes years to resolve—just might be related to the presence of a table.

Almost any negotiation will go more smoothly without a table. A table in a room is a powerful symbol, and none of the symbolism is good. By putting people on opposite sides of the table, a table literally creates a divisive barrier. It formalizes the proceedings, which stiffens people and reminds them to put on their "game face." If it's a big table in a big room, it seems to attract extra people to fill up its many seats—and additional people tend to complicate rather than simplify a negotiation.

I think you can accomplish much more outside of the traditional business environment. That's why I've always liked golf courses, restaurants, sports events, and other hospitable settings for many of my negotiations. The quasi-social environment seems to put people at ease and make them more agreeable.

I know how powerful and intoxicating atmosphere can be in a negotiation because I've seen how it affects people (including myself) when the other side is controlling the atmospherics.

A few years ago I went to a jewelry shop on New York's Fifth Avenue with a friend who was much wealthier and more interested in fine jewelry than I ever will be. Let's call him the Mogul. The Mogul wanted an emerald necklace for his wife. The store manager must have recognized the Mogul as a very serious buyer, because we were instantly ushered out of the main salon, down a series of wood-paneled corridors, and into a private room where the walls, carpeting, furnishings, and flower settings were all variations on white and beige. In this cool, hushed, virtually color-free setting, the emeralds and rubies in the display cases sparkled like klieg lights.

As the manager began bringing out emeralds of steadily increasing value for the Mogul's examination, it seemed as if all sense of reality had been vacuum-swept from the room. There was no noise, no color, no distractions from the outside world, no sense of the relative value of money in this creamy, womblike chamber. All that remained were emeralds being compared against other emeralds. Since the manager had carefully stair-stepped his presentation—each necklace was more dazzling and costly than than the one before—I suppose it was predictable that the Mogul liked the most expensive one. The price was $350,000. It was classic bump-the-customer-up salesmanship—if the Mogul had bought on the spot.

But then the Mogul did something unpredictable. He whispered to me, "I like them, but I'm not going to buy them in this room. Let's get out of here." The next day he phoned the manager and offered to buy the necklace for $125,000 less. The manager made some vain protestations about how he didn't negotiate, how his shop wasn't a Turkish bazaar, but ultimately the Mogul got his necklace at his price.

In hindsight, the manager had lost the negotiation the moment he let the Mogul out of the room.

The Mogul knew jewels. He knew what a fair price was in a business where pricing can be outrageously elastic (if not extortionate). He knew when he was being sold, which he didn't really mind inside the store. He was, after all, a customer.

But he also knew that if he wanted to negotiate on price, the setting was conspiring against him. As long as he was inside the store, the manager could always deflect his reduced offer by referring him back to jewels in a lower price range.

If the Mogul was outside the store and on the phone, the manager couldn't do that. He would have to deal with the lone issue of price. Outside the store, the Mogul would also be more objective and disciplined. The necklace wouldn't be in front of him, beguiling him with its beauty and tempting him to cave in on price. The Mogul knew once he had walked out of the store, he could also walk away from the necklace.

I mention this incident as an example of the seductive and possibly negative power of setting in a negotiation. The absence of a formal negotiating table can move things along. Of course, this might not always work to your advantage, particularly if the other side totally controls the environment.

But environment can also have a positive effect on a negotiation.

A Swiss entrepreneur once asked me to help set up a golf game outside Paris with a top French government official. My Swiss friend had sold merchandise to the government but was deadlocked on some major issues. He thought if he could get the official outside his official environment, the negotiations might improve. So he enlisted my help. I brought along a golf client whom the official admired, which made the outing special.

It was an interesting round of golf, largely because both the French official and my Swiss friend played abysmally. As the day wore on, their poor play seemed to bond them. The protocol in "transaction golf" is to be very subtle about bringing up business, if you do it at all. It's understood, not spoken. But by the 10th hole, the two men were having such a bad day that they were ready to talk about anything but golf. My Swiss friend handled this beautifully, assembling his argument with a sound bite or two on every remaining hole. By the time we reached the clubhouse, the two men had ironed out all their differences and scribbled their agreement on a cocktail napkin.

I'll never know if it was the beauty of the day that made them so agreeable or their poor play that brought them together. But I do know that getting people out of the usual business setting and placing them in a congenial environment for four or five hours will improve almost any negotiation.

If you press the issue, you'll find that most people don't want to spend their time haggling and bickering with the other side. It's not that they don't like negotiating. They like the friendly competition, the maneuvering, the development of a strategy and its execution. But more than anything, they like reaching an agreement. The less time, hassle, and confrontation, the better.

I'm sure that's what's going on when people brag about the deals they've negotiated over casual drinks or a meal or a round of golf. When they come back to the office brandishing the cocktail napkin on which the deal terms are scribbled, I often think they're more pleased about how quickly they negotiated an agreement than what the terms actually are. The cocktail napkin is a testament to their negotiating skill. Actually, it's a testament to negotiating in a casual, quasi-social setting. It's proof positive of the wisdom of getting away from the "negotiating table."

GO WITH YOUR GUT INSTINCTS, BUT GO WITH CARE

A friend's son, a young entrepreneur who has been running his own small company for the last five years, told me recently that the toughest part of his job was learning to trust his gut instincts when faced with a major decision.

He said, "I'm a victim of my business-school education. I was taught to put my faith in spreadsheets and research and decision trees and simulation programs. The more data I could collect, the smarter my decisions. The professors never told me that I'd usually be flying by the seat of my pants."

Actually, I've always thought the bigger problem was not learning to trust your gut but trusting it too much. It only takes a short string of smart decisions as you build your business—when the operation is small and the decisions are risky but relatively uncomplicated—to make you believe that you have a "golden gut," that your instincts are infallible. I've learned the hard way that you have to be selective when relying on intuition. Any skilled negotiator will tell you that each transaction is part of a continuing and humbling process of learning when to go with your gut and when to go with something more real. The following factors may give you a little more faith in your instincts.

1. IS IT A GUT DECISION OR A GUT REACTION?

A *gut decision* is the choice you face after you've collected and digested all the facts. A *gut reaction* is the same choice after you've heard only one fact.

Gut decisions can be made slowly, calmly, confidently; they are based on instinct and experience tempered by information and a broad sampling of opinion. Gut reactions are the opposite. They are made quickly, emotionally, and often irrationally; they are based on instinct that is overwhelmed by a compelling piece of information or by the heat of the moment.

You'd think most people would appreciate the difference, that they would realize the inherent danger of gut reactions and be aware of the times when they are relying on them. But people don't—with alarming frequency.

Consider the decision to purchase stock in a company, a decision that a million adults make every weekday in America. In theory, given the rules of disclosure and the blanket press coverage accorded publicly traded companies, buying a stock should be one of the most well informed decisions you can make. Yet how many people base their decision on a tip heard at dinner or a neighbor's boast that he doubled his investment in two weeks? That solitary fact gets them excited about the stock and impels them to call their broker. The same people who might spend a half hour deciding between three brands of $30 toasters in an appliance store will blithely gamble a healthy chunk of their net worth on a gut reaction.

Before you can trust your instincts, you should know whether you are deciding or merely reacting.

2. DO YOU HAVE A PRIVATE SET OF RULES?

Instinct, by definition, is not a perfect science; it's not even an imperfect science. It's an art form. You could read all the texts on game theory and decision making and still not come up with a practical set of rules about intuition. The best you can do is establish a private set of rules that make you feel comfortable and work more often than not. The tough part is sticking to your rules.

If I have a rule about gut instincts, I'd call it the "one piece missing" rule. If I'm being forced to decide in a negotiation, I always look for the one missing piece in the puzzle. It could be a big question mark about someone's character or some doubt about the other side's ability to pay, but if I spot the missing piece and no one can explain it to me, my gut tells me "no go." It's not a perfect rule, but I'm comfortable with it.

This rule doesn't apply to every negotiation. There are some situations where I'm simply not smart enough to spot the missing piece. For example, I know nothing about computers. If our people are negotiating for a $10 million upgrade to our computer network, I don't know enough to even ask smart questions. In that case, I trust our people, not my gut.

This approach also works in quasi-negotiations such as personnel decisions. If I'm considering hiring someone and there's one piece missing in his or her background—an unexplained gap in his or her employment history, a mystery about a sudden departure from his or her last job, an unenthusiastic testimonial from a reference—my gut decision is "Don't hire this person." A lot of people would overlook this missing piece or give the candidate the benefit of the doubt. They'd make a gut decision, but it's a gamble.

I'm making a gut decision too. But it's based on a personal rule that eliminates the gamble. I'm comfortable with that.

3. Are you being forced into a gut decision?

The biggest reason people make too many gut decisions is that other people force them into it. In a world where salespeople tease customers with products that are "On Sale for One Day Only," it's easy to see how we all fall into this trap. It doesn't help that the world seems to equate decisiveness with quick decisions rather than smart ones.

To reduce the number of gut decisions in a transaction, all you have to do is pause and ask yourself, "Why am I being rushed into agreeing with the other side?" If no one provides an acceptable answer to that, the only thing your gut should be telling you is "Go slow."

4. Act confidently after you go with your gut.

How you behave after you make a gut decision to accept or reject a deal is more important than what you said or did before you made it. That makes sense. If you act confidently about the agreement you created (regardless of how you truly feel), others will be confident about it too. If you (of all people!) express doubts, what reason is there for anyone else to feel confident about the transaction?

This may be the most important thing to know about trusting your instincts. Once you go with your gut, don't look back and second-guess the outcome. If you do, the rest of the world will look back with you.

THERE IS AN EDGE IN KNOWING HOW COMPANIES REALLY WORK

Fila, the Italian sportswear company, wasn't always a giant multinational enterprise. In the mid-1970s it was a fledgling organization that had pinned a great deal of its future in tennis apparel on a manufacturing and licensing relationship with our client Bjorn Borg. I've always admired how the Fila people got the most out of that relationship.

Early in the relationship the Fila people realized that the more of Borg's time they could get for promotional purposes, the better their investment. So they came up with a very clever tactic—which became known internally as "the Fila trick"—for gauging Borg's availability. They would ask the same question, usually concerning what Borg would or would not commit to in terms of time, of a half dozen people in our company. Since they were dealing with us all over the world, they got quite good at this. They would use what they were told in Australia to their best advantage in Japan; they would use what they were told in Japan to their best advantage in England; and so on in Paris, Stockholm, and Milan, until they circled the globe. ·

We were always amazed at how much the Fila people knew about Borg's schedule until we realized their secret: They had figured out a weakness in our organization—namely, that our various foreign offices didn't always talk in a coordinated fashion with one another—and used it against us.

This episode taught me an important negotiating lesson. Every organization has chinks in its organizational armor. If you can find those flaws, you can cut any organization, no matter how inscrutable or imposing it may seem to an outsider, down to size.

One corporate chink that has fascinating negotiating implications is a company's "institutional memory."

I've always thought that some of the most valuable people in a company were its "historians"—the people who have been with a company for 30 or more years and remember many of the details from an earlier era. In some cases, these veterans may not be as active or productive as they used to be, but they still provide a golden service. In meetings they can give you perspective and a historical frame of reference. If your Young Turks come up with a wild idea, it's nice to have a sage in the room who can say, with great authority, that the idea is not so new, that the company tried it 20 years ago, and then recite five reasons why it didn't work then and probably won't work now. People like this are a company's institutional memory. They are priceless.

Times change, however. With all the downsizings and early retirements, as well as the general increase in executive mobility, I've noticed that a lot of companies have lost their institutional memory. Not only are their veteran executives gone, but the people you dealt with four or five years ago have also moved to other jobs at other companies.

This struck me when a foreign publisher expressed an interest in certain rights to a five-year-old book by an author we represented. Unfortunately, the book's original publisher controlled those specific rights—and getting them back might cost us more money than we would make on the new sale. Then one of our executives made an interesting observation: None of the people involved with the book were still employed at the publishing house. The editor-in-chief who bought the book, the CEO who authorized the large check, and the editor who edited the manuscript had all moved to rival publishers. The new people there were probably so busy with their own current projects they didn't have a clue about the rights they held to the book, and they probably didn't care.

Our executive took his point a step further. With no interest in or memory of the book at the publishing house, we could probably resell the rights in question and no one would know or care. Our legal department quashed this idea immediately. But the insight emboldened us to approach the publisher about relinquishing the rights—which they did for nothing. I doubt if things would have gone so smoothly if someone involved in the original contract had still been there.

Another interesting chink is the omnipresent conflict between corporate and personal agendas.

Every company has people who have personal agendas that are not completely in sync with the company's goals. If you know that about someone at that company, you can sometimes get that person to agree to your terms merely by catering to his or her personal agenda. I know this is true because people have employed this tactic on us.

We once had a sales executive who brought in a lot of deals every year. This was a virtue and a flaw. It was a virtue because he closed a lot of sales and brought in a lot of quick revenue. It was a flaw because he was too quick to agree to the other side's price. He couldn't walk out of the room without a deal. As a result he didn't always get the best price for our clients and properties. If he were more patient, if he were willing to leave the room and wait a month or two, when the customer would be more eager, or if he were more creative about adding other features that involved other parts of our company to the deal, he could have gotten a much better price.

I blame myself in large part for the gap between his agenda and ours, because it started with the way I judged and rewarded his performance. Since I based his compensation on how much money be brought into his division, it made sense that he would only sell his division's products. If I had changed his compensation criteria to include sales he made for other parts of the company, perhaps he would have been more patient and generated bigger sales.

The interesting thing about this situation was that some of the customers he dealt with knew this about him, so they went out of their way to deal with him rather than with our other executives who drove harder bargains. It was a chink in our armor, and for a few years a few observant outsiders benefited from it.

"TALENT" SHOULD NEVER TOUCH THE MONEY

One of the less appreciated blessings of our client management business over the years has been the minimal amount of interference we get from our clients. We don't tell our superstars how to read a nickel defense or hit a topspin lob, and they in turn don't lecture us about how to structure a deal or sell their services.

I was reminded of this not-so-tiny blessing the other day by one of our young executives who wanted some guidance about a client who keeps insisting on sitting in on business meetings.

There are three situations when the client should tag along:

(A) WHEN THE CLIENT KNOWS MORE THAN YOU DO.
Theoretically, you should be smarter than your clients. If not, why do they need you? But I can envision situations where the client should be in the room. If I am negotiating a merchandising agreement for a new electronic gadget, it may be a big advantage for me to have the gadget's inventor in the room. I may know a lot about merchandising, but the client is the expert on how the gadget works.

(B) WHEN THE CLIENT HAS A PERSONAL RELATIONSHIP WITH THE OTHER SIDE.
It's always nice to do business with friends. If these friends feel a personal attachment to your client, they might be more accommodating on certain points if the client is present.

(C) WHEN THE CLIENT'S STATURE CAN CLOSE THE DEAL.
Sometimes the presence of a superstar client in a meeting can force the other side's hand. We could be going back and forth for months negotiating a deal for a superstar athlete. But if we bring the superstar to the next meeting, his presence somehow has a galvanizing effect on the discussion. Everyone is more alert, more serious, and more accommodating. After all, it's one thing for the other side to tell me, "Your superstar isn't worth the price you're asking." It's another for them to say it to the superstar's face.

Having said that, however, I firmly believe that "talent"—and this means everyone from athletes to performing artists to authors to broadcasters to cartoonists—should stay out of business deals.

For one thing, their time is better spent perfecting their particular sport, art, or craft. That's what makes them unique. Lots of people can negotiate a contract. Only a few can hit a tennis ball like Pete Sampras or sing a Puccini aria like Kiri Te Kanawa.

I also think it's potentially dispiriting for "talent," particularly performers and creative people, to deal with hard money issues. It can create a barrier between "talent" and audience. My rule is, Talent should never touch the money. I even apply it to myself. I'm an experienced businessman, but when I function as an author or lecturer, I let other people negotiate the financial terms of a personal appearance. I don't touch the money because I don't want any ill will that may have arisen in the negotiation to intrude on the goodwill I want to generate during my speech.

Moreover, most talented people are temperamentally unsuited for the unique give-and-take that constitutes a business transaction. Although I've known athletes who are very shrewd and successful businesspeople, my general experience has been that a killer instinct on the playing field doesn't always translate into a killer instinct at the negotiating table. The rules in business are not as well defined as they are in, say, golf or tennis. Athletes who have always played within the rules can't always appreciate or understand that some businesspeople play everything close to or even over the line.

I learned this early on with Arnold Palmer, who by training and inclination has always operated within a strict and narrow code. Arnold had been raised in a family that stressed all the noble and forthright virtues, especially in business.

You did not lay your cards on the table; you started with them there. Arnold had no use for the maneuverings and subtleties of negotiation. He considered them at best to be a waste of time and at worst a deceit. He did not appreciate the need for getting up and walking out of a room when things were not going well or for telling someone a deal is off when you do not really mean it is off at all. And he could not abide the occasional use of a raised voice. As a lawyer, trained to be a vocal adversary, I regarded a heated debate as part of the negotiating process. As a golfer, trained to be a sportsman and gentleman, Arnold considered a raised voice a personal affront and a call to arms.

Arnold and I once had dinner in Chicago with an entrepreneur who had an idea for a television show requiring Arnold's participation. As we discussed terms, the exchange between the entrepreneur and me became testy. Sharp words flew across the table. Arnold watched us go at it, feeling genuine embarrassment for us, as if he had been trapped in an ugly domestic quarrel. I'm sure he understood that part of it was posturing on my part, but the scene still made him uncomfortable. As we left the restaurant, Arnold turned to me and said, "Don't ever get me into anything like that again, Mark. I was about to hit that man right in the mouth."

I have tried to follow that admonition ever since.

Keeping the client out of the room is also a selling advantage. It is far easier to extol a superstar's talents and virtues when the superstar is not present. The last thing I need in a negotiation where I am ardently selling the client's talents is to have that client making modest, self-deprecating noises from the corner of the room. While it may humanize the client, it totally undercuts my negotiating position.

Clients also can destroy the logic and pattern of a negotiation. They interrupt. They freely answer questions that are none of the other side's business. They are not skilled at masking their true thoughts. Even in my earliest days, I liked to have a certain order for presenting topics in a negotiation. But I noticed that whenever Arnold Palmer or Gary Player or Jack Nicklaus sat in on the meeting, they were just as likely to answer questions and alter the pattern that I thought was best for the negotiation. (In many cases, this wasn't altogether their fault; the other side would shrewdly turn to them rather than deal with me.) I eventually learned that leaving clients out of the bargaining sessions was actually doing them a favor.

Of course, the best reason to keep "talent" out of the transaction is to give yourself a fallback position on any negotiating point. When the other side poses a tough question that you do not want to answer at that specific moment, you cannot say, "I'll have to check with my client" if he or she is sitting next to you.

THE BENEFITS OF WORKING WITHOUT A CONTRACT

Given the choice in a business transaction, which would you prefer—a person's word or his or her signature on a contract?

One of our younger executives recently approached me with this problem. For the past six weeks, she had been working on a project for an important customer—without a contract. The client assured her that our company had the job and that their legal department would get to the paperwork. But she wasn't sure. "How," she wanted to know, "do we get them to sign before we put so much work into the project that they're calling all the shots and we can't turn back?"

Working without a contract happens a lot more often in business than you imagine. And like our young executive, many people don't fully appreciate the benefits of doing so.

For one thing, if you have worked with the customer before, your risk is minimal. They obviously like working with you. If they're honorable people, they'll keep their word. If they're not honorable, I doubt if any contract will bind them or fully protect you. (And why would you be dealing with them anyway?)

But more important, as the selling party, you're not the only one at risk without a contract. The buyer is, too—because the more work you do for the buyer, the more obligated he or she will feel toward you.

Over the years we have frequently worked for months on projects without a signed agreement. There have been instances when we have gone into the second year of a transaction before we had a signed contract for the first year. My 30-year relationship with Arnold Palmer is based on a handshake.

I don't say this to minimize the importance of contracts. They can be quite handy when people don't do what they're supposed to do. But I don't want to minimize the value of a person's word.

A person's word is a matter of honor. A contract is a matter of law. Assuming you've performed creditably and behaved honorably, when honor is the issue, the other side will go to great lengths to be more than fair to you.

I advised our junior executive to keep on working. Eventually some money would change hands (if only to cover

our expenses). There would also be some correspondence between the customer and us that could be construed as legally
binding. But most important, the more work we did for them,
the more we would know about their business and the more
they would like us. You can't buy that kind of leverage and
goodwill—or mandate it with a contract.

A beverage company once asked us to create a series of
sporting events in 12 major markets. Our fee for setting up
the events would be $10,000 per city. Rather than wait for a
fully executed contract, our people did a whirlwind tour of
all 12 cities, scouting venues, talking to distributors, and lin-
ing up promotional support. We knew from past experience
that booking up venues well in advance (instead of at the last
minute) would save the client considerable money.

A few weeks later the client had second thoughts. They
wanted only six markets—which represented a loss of $60,000
in fees to us. Fortunately, we didn't have a contract.

We reminded the client of all the work we had already
done and the money we had saved them by acting quickly in
good faith based on their assurances. Because we were deeply
into the project, we also were more knowledgeable about certain markets than they were.

Although we couldn't convince the beverage company to
sponsor events in all 12 markets as originally planned, they
eventually visited nine.

But having seen how hard we worked, they made us whole
by increasing our per-market fee. I'm not sure their lawyers
or business affairs people would have permitted that if there
had been a contract.

KNOW YOUR NEGOTIATING STYLE— AND THE OTHER SIDE'S, TOO

What's your negotiating style? Do you have to have all the i's dotted and t's crossed before you feel you have a deal?

Or are you comfortable agreeing to the broad outlines of a transaction, proceeding as if you have a deal and worrying about the details later?

There's nothing inherently right or wrong about either negotiating technique. You'll find successful practitioners of both in business every day. The problem occurs when opposing styles collide, when two negotiators go up against each other—one very strict, the other more loose and trusting—and they're not aware of the difference!

I happen to be a fairly loose negotiator. I'll make the big deal and worry about the details later. I wasn't always like this, until I realized that "getting it done," not "getting it written down," is the true key to staying in business.

I learned this years ago in the same "golf challenge" deal with MCA that I mentioned in chapter 3. MCA agreed to produce 12 golf shows a year for network television featuring my clients Arnold Palmer and Gary Player. We were into the second year of the agreement before we ever signed the first year's contract.

Being trained as a lawyer, I hadn't realized that this was how the entertainment industry sometimes worked. Then I got to thinking about the business implications of this practice. Here we were painstakingly trying to resolve all the terms of a standard 80-page contract, but MCA had already agreed to our gut issues—Palmer and Player would receive their fee up front for each program as well as a percentage of foreign rights. The rest of the contract was relatively unimportant.

It seemed to me that MCA had outsmarted themselves. We made the programs. MCA paid Arnold and Gary. Meanwhile, MCA had its investment tied up in production costs. If something went wrong, they had much more to lose than my clients. Thus, by getting the deal done (though not signed), we held all the trump cards.

Fortunately, because both of us had the same negotiating approach, it was the best kind of leverage—the kind we never had to use.

You can't expect the same friendly outcome when negotiating styles clash.

I remember our attempt to acquire a sports marketing operation in Europe, which foundered because we didn't pay enough attention to the negotiator we assigned to the acquisition.

The executive who handled the deal was a classic detail man with a negotiating routine that I thought would be appropriate for a potentially complex deal. He liked to resolve the big issues first. Then he would move on to the smaller points. He didn't discriminate among major or minor points. They all got his undivided attention, as if each were the most crucial item in the world. But once he resolved an issue, he moved on to the next point, and so on down the line until he was fully satisfied.

The entrepreneur who owned the company was the direct opposite. He was a quick deal maker who was notorious for tinkering with the details later on. I thought sending one of our steadiest, most focused executives could counter this entrepreneur's slipperiness. I thought wrong.

After several weeks of friendly sparring, our executive reported that we had a deal. A week later, it fell apart—not because one side had changed its mind but because of the two men's differing approaches to the details.

The deal breaker was a disagreement about which side would settle a few outstanding overhead costs. The money involved was minimal, a fraction of the deal. But our negotiator, the detail man, regarded this point as settled and written in stone; he would not budge. The entrepreneur, who was adept at smoothing out the details to fit the deal, expected us to yield.

The transaction quickly self-destructed over this miniscule budget item, but the root cause was two businesspeople's intransigent and incompatible negotiating styles.

ARE YOU GUILTY OF "PERFECT MATH"?

Two associates of mine were recently discussing cost cutting in our New York operation. The item at hand was an apartment we keep in town for visiting clients. One associate contended that we could make money on the apartment if, as she said, "we could put a client in the apartment every week of the year and charge them $500 per week. Multiply that by 52 weeks and the $26,000 would cover the rent." She used the same calculus for several other items, to the point where the apartment looked like a potential profit center.

An associate cut her off, saying, "That sounds good, but you're using perfect math. I seriously doubt if the apartment will be full each week."

I liked that phrase *perfect math*, because it summed up all the false or inflated assumptions that pollute our decision making each day. I think we're all guilty of perfect math in one way or another when we start off with an attractive number or fact and use that as the basis for an uninterrupted chain of events to achieve a stated goal. The truth of the matter is that it usually doesn't work out that way. Even if we start off with fairly sound assumptions, things rarely fall into place as neatly as we would like them.

The best negotiators are always vigilant for signs of perfect math—in themselves as well as others—and they use these signs to improve, not cloud, their judgment.

For over 20 years, anyone who has ever come to me with an invention in golf has exhibited the same reasoning to persuade me to invest in it. The logic is so familiar I can recite it in my sleep. "There are 10 million avid golfers in America," they tell me. "If we can just get 10 percent of them to buy our practice device, on which we make $12 per unit, we'll be making $12 million."

Sounds great, doesn't it? But that's precisely the kind of argument that scares me. The numbers are so rosy and the assumptions so casual that I know I never want to do business with the inventor. Even when he or she discounts the response rate to a more realistic number—say, 2 percent rather than 10 percent—I'm still unimpressed.

I would feel a little more confident if the inventor were less confident about his or her numbers. Just once I'd like someone to walk into my office and tell me that he or she recognizes how hard it is to make these numbers work out.

- **Does he or she know how hard it is to identify and reach those "10 million avid golfers"?**

- Is he or she aware of all the manufacturing glitches that can eat into that $12-per-unit profit margin?

- What about competitors with similar products?

In other words, just once I'd like to hear an inventor admit he or she is working with imperfect math.

The easiest way to counter the argument that you're using perfect math, of course, is to back it up with real-world facts. A golf inventor's credibility would soar in my eyes if he or she walked into my office with the results of a test mailing proving his or her desired response rate, or if the inventor had called on six pro shops and each had ordered 100 of the new devices.

It's amazing how many people forget this.

When There's Nothing to Do, Do It Brilliantly

More than anything else, I think patience is *the* most vital negotiating skill and its absence the most deadly negotiating error. I have seen countless negotiations turn into lopsided messes or fall apart completely because of impatience, but I can't recall a negotiation that ended unhappily for us because of the shrewd, calculated exercise of patience.

Patience comes in many forms. It's knowing that pushing too hard or too fast to resolve a deal point can turn the other side off or drive them away. It's resisting the myriad pressures to "get a deal done" (a deadline, a quota, a "what have you done for me lately" client, a boss looking over your shoulder) because you know that hastily conceding a "minor" point without thinking it through can transform it into a major point later on. It's walking away from the negotiation until the other side comes to their senses. But more than anything else, patience is doing nothing.

The key, of course, is recognizing those situations when there's nothing to do—and doing it brilliantly.

I recall a few years ago when one of our clients, a popular American sportscaster, became the object of an intense bidding war among three American television networks. I'd like to say that we orchestrated a grand scheme that, to borrow a phrase from investment bankers, put this sportscaster "in play." But, in truth, it was sheer happenstance that brought the three networks to his door. Nevertheless, with three well-heeled suitors feverishly bidding for our client's services, we realized we were in an enviable position.

The logical next step would have been to take advantage of this frenzy, to heat up the competition. We knew how to do that. We could formalize the bidding process. We could outline what our client was looking for in his next "home." We could set deadlines. We could ask for detailed proposals. We could set up an auction and watch the networks try to knock each other out. We could work the phones with the press, which would do its part to add a few more degrees of heat and confusion to the process. We could haul out all the weapons in our negotiating arsenal to pit the networks against one another.

Instead, we did nothing, which was the correct move under the circumstances.

For one thing, our client was a very private and dignified individual. He didn't want his contract negotiation to become a public spectacle, which could easily have happened if we had executed all our standard negotiating tactics.

We were also a little nervous about the chaos and frenzy the networks were displaying over our client. Chaos can be good. It can bring about quick and sweeping change, not only in where our clients work but in how much they get paid. The trouble with chaos, though, is that you rarely can control it. Only a soothsayer or fool thinks he or she can predict and control events when everyone else is running around dazed and confused. Tempting as it may be to join the fray, it's sometimes better to sit on the sidelines and wait for the dust to settle.

So we adopted a passive posture. We listened.

We listened as each network representative made an offer to our client.

Our response to each was, "Thank you. We'll consider it."

Then we waited for the networks' impatience to grow. We kept in touch, of course. As new ideas came to mind, we would occasionally call up the networks to chat about our client, to float an idea, or to let them know that he was still interested if something could be worked out. But at no point did we formalize a negotiating process or indicate that a bidding war was in progress.

This went on for weeks, during which time our client was perfectly happy fulfilling his broadcasting duties for his current employer. Then, like a miler breaking away from the pack in the final lap of a race, one of the networks decided to end the process with a record-breaking offer that we could not (and did not) refuse. In the end, our client quadrupled his salary, and it was all done quietly and privately.

It could be argued that, as negotiators, we had it easy. We stumbled into a bidding war because we had a client whom everyone wanted. We were in the catbird seat. We couldn't lose.

That's true. But in my mind, that makes our passive, wait-and-see approach even more impressive.

An experienced card player will tell you that getting the most out of a really strong hand sometimes requires more skill than winning with very little. It's no different in a business negotiation. Some people become incredibly error-prone when they hold all the strong cards. They move too quickly or overplay their hand. They irritate people and let players get out of the game.

In that sense, we did "nothing"—and we did it brilliantly. Just because you're watching and listening doesn't mean you aren't planning and maneuvering. It doesn't mean you are not negotiating.

NEGOTIATING THE FOUR PHASES OF A CLIENT'S CAREER

Any marketing textbook will teach you that there are four stages in the development of a product or brand: introduction, growth, maturity, and decline. But I seriously wonder how many people fully appreciate these four phases and factor them into their negotiating approach.

I've been in negotiations where the other side has behaved as if their product or service were still in the robust growth phase of the cycle—when even the most casual observer knew that it was more accurately somewhere between maturity and decline. As a result, the other side took a more aggressive negotiating posture than they deserved—and consequently drove me away. That's not good negotiating.

Not surprisingly, these four phases also apply to the career and marketability of an athlete—and they significantly dictate

113

how we negotiate for that client and even who we choose to do the negotiating.

1. INTRODUCTION

The introduction or start-up phase of an athlete's life is fairly simple. He or she starts competing, hopefully does well, and captures the attention of aficionados in the sport. As negotiators in this phase, our job is to create a positive groundswell of interest in the athlete, laying the groundwork for the first two or three commercial contracts.

In my experience, a negotiator's most important attribute here is *credibility*. It's the foundation for everything that follows. That's why I always try to include a senior person from our company in the negotiating mix for a budding star athlete. A senior person has the credibility not only to make bold statements about the athlete (and, hence, bold demands) but also to make them stick.

For example, if I told a wide variety of people that a promising young golfer was going to be the best I've ever seen, merely by saying that I could probably negotiate a slew of contracts for that golfer—because I have some credibility. I've been around the game for a long time, I've been involved with some of the great players, and I have a track record that suggests my prediction is just as likely to be right as wrong. That same statement might not carry as much weight with potential customers if it came from a junior person in our golf division.

A negotiator also needs a keen appreciation of the *short term*. In the start-up phase, you do not want to tie up your client interminably in long-term contracts. There's a limit to how much money you can get if you're selling the promise of someone who is *going to be a superstar*. That limit is considerably higher if your client is an *established superstar*.

For example, if your client has just been named Rookie of the Year in the National Basketball Association, it might be tempting to sign a multimillion-dollar shoe deal for 10 years with powerhouse companies such as Reebok or Nike. These two shoe companies are very competitive, and they're always looking to throw money at "the next big thing" in sports and lock him or her up in long-term arrangements.

But 10 years is a long time. If your client continues to improve in the NBA, what looks like a good shoe deal now may seem paltry in 10 years when he is one of NBC's marquee attractions. You can try to renegotiate in the middle of the contract, but you rarely do so from a position of strength. In the start-up phase, you're better off with short-term contracts—with renewal clauses and escalating payments that reward your client for doing what everyone expects him or her to do.

2. GROWTH

The growth phase should be the most lucrative and the most fun for a negotiator. Your client is an established megastar. You're in a seller's market with the name that everyone wants to be associated with. Your phone is ringing off the hook. You're reacting to offers rather than proactively seeking them out. It should be an easy life, but it rarely is.

A negotiator's most important skill in the growth phase is maintaining quality control. You've inherited a cash cow but you don't want to milk it dry. You need to insulate your client from all the distractions and pressures that attractive business opportunities present. When people throw money at an athlete, they're paying for three things: name, image, and time. Name and image are easy to supply. Time is a problem, especially when an athlete would be better off practicing, improving, and continuing to win rather than making commercials or shaking hands at a store opening. In other words, in this phase a negotiator needs to know *how to say no*.

Saying no also requires a negotiator to make some personal sacrifices. With so many people making demands on the client's time, it's impossible for the client to say yes to all of them. Likewise, it's not in the client's best interest to personally tell people no (because that's not what a friendly, agreeable, popular athlete who owes good fortune to his or her adoring public does). It's the manager's job to say no. The manager is the bad cop in a good cop/bad cop relationship (the client, of course, is always the good cop), and he or she must be willing to play that role without hesitation.

Consequently, a negotiator must also develop a very thick skin in the growth phase. We once had a tennis player who had a marvelous way of dealing with press requests. Without exception, she would tell media people she would be delighted to appear on their radio show or be interviewed for their magazine. That was her automatic response. "Just call IMG and they'll arrange it," she would say, all smiles and charm. Within seconds, she would be on the phone instructing her manager to say no when the station or magazine called to schedule the interview.

A good negotiator accepts the fact that you can't please everyone in the growth phase.

3. MATURITY

The most important skill in the mature phase may be simply *recognizing that you are in it.*

If you're marketing a bar of soap, it's easy to tell if the product is mature. It's there in the sales figures. If sales have hit a plateau or you're losing market share over several years, your soap is mature.

It's different with athletes. Not only do they think the growth phase will never end, but they often deny that there is any diminution in their athletic skills or marketability, no matter what the scoreboard or tournament winnings say.

Maturity is not necessarily a problem for an athlete's marketability. But as a negotiator you have to prepare the athlete and yourself for the transition from Phase Two to Phase Three.

Ben Hogan, for example, would never play on the Senior Golf tour because that meant acknowledging that he wasn't a competitor on the regular tour. He didn't want to participate as a Grand Old Man of Golf. That sort of competitive fire explains a lot about his success as a golfer. But I think he lost a lot from that decision—personally as well as commercially. He didn't view playing the Masters in Augusta, Georgia, as an occasion to see old friends and enjoy a beautiful golf course. He would play only if he thought he could win. He never recognized the mature phase he was in and that people had different expectations of Ben Hogan.

4. DECLINE

Although none of our superstar clients have reached this phase yet, I believe athletes can still do well long after their athletic skills have faded. The key is to position their so-called decline more attractively as their *reflective phase*—and negotiate accordingly.

Byron Nelson in golf and Jack Kramer in tennis are two prime examples of superstars in the reflective phase. Even into their eighth and ninth decades of life, they remain ambassadors for their sports. They have tournaments and equipment named after them. They write books and articles about the game. They provide broadcast commentary at events. As elder statesmen, they have the credibility and authority to make strong and provocative statements that uphold the standards of their sports.

Unlike a bar of soap, which is not pleasant to manage in the decline phase, a legendary athlete in his or her reflective years can be a wonderful negotiating opportunity.

MYTHS ABOUT YOUR COMPANY THAT WORK TO YOUR ADVANTAGE

If you're in business long enough and attain a modicum of visibility or market leadership, eventually some preconceptions develop about your company. People, particularly your competitors, might say you charge too much, you're not what you used to be, your people are too aggressive or too hung up on details, or you're too big.

The tendency, when you're confronted with these myths, is to explain them, apologize for them, or disown them.

I disagree. Some myths about your company are more complimentary than insulting and give you a negotiating advantage. When competitors describe you in aggressive terms, at times your best response is, "Thank you." Consider these three.

1. THE MYTH THAT YOU CHARGE TOO MUCH

In our organization, we certainly charge at the top of the line, but we give very good value for what we do. Being labeled pricey in any business—whether you're a lawyer or carpenter or restaurateur or dry cleaner—is a canard if you also happen to be among the best.

The trouble with dispelling this myth is that you have to lower your prices to do so. And that's almost always disastrous. Even if there is no deterioration in service, the lower price will suggest there is. It's a matter of perception.

The truth is, people will pay a little more (sometimes a lot more) for the perceived value of dealing with the best. For example, the very best restaurants *do* charge too much, but they never lack customers. Patrons continue to pay because they know that the cheese will be properly aged, the soufflé perfect, the wine excellent, the service impeccable. They get an excellent return on a low-risk investment. They'd rather plunk down $60 per person on a guaranteed four-star experience than gamble $40 per person on the chance of eating a four-star meal at a two-star establishment.

Another point to consider: It is much easier for your competition to enter at the lower end of the price curve than to challenge you at the top.

2. THE MYTH THAT ALL CONFLICTS OF INTEREST ARE BAD

You hear this often in the financial community. An investment bank, for example, representing one company might suggest a sale of corporate assets to another client. The fact that the bank knows what both clients want, acting in effect as a broker between the two, doesn't necessarily imply that the bank has conflicting interests—certainly not if both clients are aware and approve of the bank's unique position.

In our business, people often wondered how we could represent both Chris Evert and Martina Navratilova when they were constantly battling one another to be number one. Isn't that a conflict? And yet by representing these two top tennis players, we can create opportunities for them both where one plus one equals three.

If you have a dual relationship that serves the interests of all parties, you should certainly disclose it. But don't disown it.

3. THE MYTH THAT YOU'RE TOUGH

Never dispel a reputation for toughness, deserved or not. It is invaluable in a negotiation, because the opposition is not surprised when you are tough but glad to be disappointed when you're not.

We got a reputation for toughness early on, frankly because athletes at the time were pushovers. They had no idea what they were doing and the companies that signed them were accustomed to easy, extremely favorable contracts. When we came in and started pushing for deals for our athlete clients that were closer to fair value, people labeled us tough.

I can't help thinking this myth has given us an edge over the years, especially when customers find out how reasonable we are.

ARE YOU TOUGH ENOUGH TO BE AN "EASY SELL"?

In a black-and-white world, I suppose we could divide all buyers into two camps: tough customers and easy sells.

The tough customers do all sorts of things to drive a salesperson mad. They are uncommunicative. They don't respond quickly to your letters or calls. They challenge you on every deal point. They revisit points that you thought had already been resolved. They shamelessly play you off against your competition. They're slow to pay. They're never satisfied. They turn a negotiating process that should have been wrapped up in two weeks into a four-month war. The only thing that keeps you going back to them is the fact that, in the end, they *buy*.

The easy sells are a salesperson's holiday. They say yes or no quickly. They don't hide from you when you call. They want the best price, but they know you have to make a profit too. They don't make you beg them for payment.

Of these two types, which would you rather be? And which would you prefer to negotiate with?

The paradox is that a lot of people choose the former rather than the latter. They don't want to be known as easy sells. They carefully nurture their tough-guy reputation and take pride in bullying their suppliers and vendors in every negotiation. Yet in the long run, I have a hunch the easy sells end up with the better deals.

An executive I know has a theory that difficult people are relatively more ineffective as buyers because the people selling to them make them pay a premium price for being difficult.

"If I'm trying to sell you something," he contends, "and you're hard to reach and it takes eons to close the sale and

121

you beat me up on every point, I'm going to find some way—not now but maybe later—to inflate my price. If you're this difficult now, you're going to be difficult every step of the way and I'm going to need that extra money as protection."

I'm not sure I totally buy into his logic. No matter how unpleasant they may be, short of doing something illegal, immoral, or unethical, tough negotiators are usually doing their job. They're expected to try to extract the best possible terms for themselves. Salespeople shouldn't punish them for it, certainly not by surreptitiously padding the bill. That's a sharp practice I cannot endorse.

Having said that, however, I hasten to add that tough negotiators do irritating things for which a smart salesperson can and should "make them pay."

The most irritating customers in my mind are the ones who are unresponsive and impossible to reach when you need them. The good news for a salesperson is that you can turn a customer's unresponsiveness into a tremendous negotiating edge—and you can do it in writing. The weapon of choice is a simple confirmation letter.

Most sales are usually closed by a handshake or verbal agreement, even though there are dozens of variables that have to be worked out as you draft a contract or implement the sale. Quite often a shrewd customer will be intentionally very slow to iron out these variables, because the further along the sale progresses, the more leverage he has to resolve these variables in his favor. After all, it is generally easier for a buyer to walk away from a purchase than for a salesperson (with bosses and sales quotas hovering nearby) to walk away from a sale.

A confirmation letter is the best way to handle this type of customer.

To put it in terms all of us can relate to, let's say I want you to come and work for me in New York. I broad-brush the essentials: You will be an account executive, you start on July 1, 1995, and your base salary is $50,000. You say yes. We both think we have a deal.

But we haven't talked about your vacation, your health insurance, the size of your office, your support staff, and other niceties that may be more important to you than to me. As your start date approaches, however, it is impossible for you to reach me. I never return your calls.

But the job is yours.

The smartest thing you can do with someone like me is write a letter confirming all the niceties as you see them: "I'm delighted we'll be working together. It is my understanding that I get three weeks' vacation, an office decoration allowance, a secretary . . ." If I never respond to that letter to dispute you, those terms hang there as if I've accepted them.

It's no different in a sales negotiation. If the customer is unresponsive, write to him: "I'm delighted you've bought our product. We will ship by December 1. Two-thirds of the shipment will be blue, one-third will be gray. You pay on delivery. If the product is unsatisfactory, you have seven days to return it. . . ." Again, if the customer doesn't object to your terms, the implication is that they have been has accepted. That's the way to discipline a difficult customer.

My goal here, though, is not to promote some sharp practices for salespeople. My message is directed to the negotiators on the other side, the customers. I think a lot of people have the misconception that being "easy to sell to" is somehow a pejorative. Not true. More often than not, it works to your advantage to be a gracious and pliant customer, because the seller will be more gracious and pliant with you.

If you think that constantly putting the seller through the wringer is a smart strategy, watch out. The seller has some strategies that he or she can just as easily turn on you.

• • •
THE MCCORMACK RULES

• When you listen to the other side outlining their position, you should always be thinking, "Says who?"

• Every time you let the other side go unchallenged in quoting a price, setting a deadline, dictating a procedure, or determining who says yes or no, you are letting the other side make a unilateral decision. You are letting the other side write the rules of the negotiation (rules that surely won't be written to your advantage).

• Almost any negotiation will go more smoothly without a negotiating table.

• When relying on intuition, be extremely selective. It only takes a short string of smart decisions to make you believe that you have a "golden gut" and that your instincts are infallible.

- A gut decision is the choice you face after you've collected and digested all the facts. A gut reaction is the same choice after you've heard only one fact.

- How you behave after you make a gut decision to accept or reject a deal is more important that what you said or did before you made it.

- Every organization has chinks in its organizational armor. If you can find those flaws, you can cut any organization, no matter how inscrutable or imposing it may seem to an outsider, down to size.

- Some myths about your company are more complimentary that insulting and give you a negotiating advantage. When competitors describe you in aggressive terms, sometimes your best response is, "Thank you."

- Never dispel a reputation for toughness, deserved or not. It is invaluable in a negotiation, because the opposition is not surprised when you are tough but glad to be disappointed when you're not.

CHAPTER 5

The Theory and Practice
of Thinking Big

***

FIVE REASONS PEOPLE DON'T THINK BIG

One of our London sales executives did a spectacular deal not long ago. He had elicited a seven-figure commitment from a sponsor on a project for which I thought we would be lucky to get £100,000. Like any manager, I love surprises on the upside, so I went out of my way to track him down and congratulate him. It wasn't that a seven-figure sum is such a novelty at our company. Rather, it was that I had never associated that sort of number with him.

When we finally spoke, he credited it all to his boss. "He told me not to be afraid to ask for a big number," he said. "This company was looking to do something big, so I should think big."

I loved that. If I had only two words to describe the optimal negotiating style, these would be my mantra: *Think big.*

127

It should be apparent from this example that I am impressed by people who can confound expectations and extract big numbers in a negotiation. The bigger the numbers, the more I'm impressed. It's not the only thing that impresses me, but if you run your business as a true meritocracy (and you should!), you can't go wrong honoring and rewarding people who think big.

I think there is an unspoken caste system in any organization based on whether you think big or small or somewhere in between. It's hard to put a finger on it, but the quality and magnitude of person's clients, customers, and transactions is certainly a telling sign.

Some people will always traffic in small deals. If, on a scale of 1 to 10, 10 is a megadeal in their business, their transactions will always be 3s and 4s. Other people are very comfortable around big numbers; their deals are 7s and 8s, with the occasional 10.

It's always fascinated me that the people who do the size-10 deals are just as capable of doing the 3s and 4s. But the people who do 3s and 4s can't pull off a 10. They can't clear the hurdle to a higher level.

It's not because they're dumb. (I've known too many high-IQ types who always get the short end of a negotiation to trust that excuse.)

It's not because they lack an adversarial personality. (I've been outnegotiated too many times by people whose chief weapons are niceness and charm to put too much faith in steeliness of character.)

Thinking big and, in turn, doing bigger deals is a matter of attitude. It's a matter of knowing and believing that your product or service is worth it and then overcoming all the mental blocks that force us to think small. Here are five reasons people don't think big.

1. THEY DON'T KNOW WHAT BIG IS.

The great film director Billy Wilder tells a story of his first meeting in Hollywood with detective novelist Raymond Chandler, author of *The Big Sleep*. Wilder wanted Chandler to help him write the screenplay of *Double Indemnity*.

Chandler was in his 50s but new to the screenwriting trade. He was a crotchety fellow, proud of his erudition and the Latin and Greek he had learned at an English public school, Dulwich. He wore tweed jackets with leather-patched elbows and smoked a pipe. He was extremely suspicious of the flashy, wanton ways of Hollywood and commensurately naive.

Upon meeting Wilder and his producer, Joe Sistrom, Chandler immediately announced that he would have to be paid $150 a week. Sistrom said they had expected to pay him $750. Chandler then added that it might take him two or possibly three weeks to finish a script. Wilder pointed out that writing scripts often took six months and that Chandler would be on salary for as long as necessary.

To their credit, Wilder and Sistrom called in a talent agent to protect Chandler from them and himself.

Not every negotiator is so obliging when we betray our ignorance of industry parameters.

2. THEY ARE LOCKED IN THE PAST.

Although age and experience should be advantages to a negotiator, they can be an obstacle, particularly when people don't adapt as quickly as they age.

I don't represent individual golfers anymore, but in the 1960s I represented three of the all-time greatest—Arnold Palmer, Gary Player, and Jack Nicklaus. I negotiated all their contracts, including endorsements with various equipment manufacturers around the world. We created breakthrough contracts in those days, not only in terms of financial guarantees but royalty structures, auditing procedures, definition of territories, and protection for the athletes. The sums we generated were considered huge at the time.

If I were selling golf equipment endorsements today, I'd be influenced by what was happening 25 years ago. The mere thought of a golfer making $500,000 a year to play with a certain set of clubs would not come easily to someone like me who started out in an era when $30,000 a year was mindboggling. It's not that I'm not aware of changes in the golf club industry or haven't kept up with the going rate for top golfers today, but it's hard to let go of past triumphs. Without my negotiating baggage, a younger executive might come at it from a different and fresher perspective and push the envelope a little harder. Quite often that's the difference between thinking big and bigger.

Thus, in 1990 another executive at our company negotiated Greg Norman's golf club contract with Cobra. Since Cobra was a start-up operation that couldn't afford Norman's customary endorsement fee, he negotiated for and got an equity position in Cobra that has already paid Norman a huge multiple of what he could earn in fees and royalties.

3. They look behind them for guidance.

This is a variation on being trapped in the past. Where some people let past examples define what is big and what isn't, others use the past not only to color but to dictate their negotiating approach.

We face this in our business all the time when a contract is up for renewal. Let's say a television network has bought the broadcast rights to a sports event for three years with escalating fees of $1 million in year one, $1.2 million in year two, and $1.45 million in year three. That's a 20 percent increase each year. When the contract expires, we could renegotiate a new three-year deal with the same 20 percent annual increase. That might not be bad. After all, we haven't lost ground. We will have doubled our fee by year five, and how many other businesses grow 20 percent every year?

It might not be bad, but it's not thinking big. Thinking big would be shooting for a 21 percent increase—or more. Thinking big would be limiting the renewal to one year because we know another network will soon be interested in the event (and adding a competitor to the mix usually works to our advantage). Thinking big might be finding out what other networks are paying for equivalent properties and adding a 20 percent premium to those figures to come up with our new fee.

Thinking big comes in many forms, but it doesn't slavishly use previous deals as the frame of reference for future negotiations. If you're thinking big, the only use you have for past negotiations is to stand them on their head.

4. THEY WANT TO BE IN THE GAME AT ANY COST.

We have an executive who by any measure is comfortable with big numbers. On the proverbial 1-to-10 scale, some of the deals he has negotiated would classify as 12s or 13s. Given the right client or property, he can deliver numbers that are off the charts. He is a shrewd and tenacious advocate on behalf of a client. He doesn't care what the other side thinks of him or his tactics. He has his eye on the prize; he doesn't need to be liked.

But he becomes unrecognizably timid when he negotiates a fee for his own services. In our business, before you can represent a client, you have to convince the client that we provide the best representation. You have to sell your services and negotiate payment for those services. In the athlete representation side of our business, the fee structure is well established and firm. There's not much room for flexibility. There are standard commissions that we stick to.

We also represent the various commercial rights—from broadcasting to marketing to merchandising—to major sports events. When the 1994 Winter Olympics were shown on television, our company was the one negotiating those broadcast rights with the dozens of television networks around the world on behalf of the organizing committee in Lillehammer, Norway. We've done the same for most Olympic organizing committees since the 1980 games as well as for countless other events, governing bodies, and sports federations.

Our compensation for this sort of consulting varies, depending on the work we have to do. Sometimes we get a flat fee. Sometimes we work for a fixed commission. Sometimes the commission increases as we exceed specific revenue targets. But in each case, we have to negotiate our compensation.

Here's where this executive forgets to think big. Time and again, he has sold his talents and our company's resources cheap, getting a fraction of what other people would get for the same consulting.

I have several theories why.

Part of it, I'm sure, is the difference between negotiating for someone else and for yourself. It's easier to argue that someone else's product is "the best in the world" and worth top dollar than it is to say it about yourself. The former is advocacy, the latter braggadocio.

Part of it might be that he's such a natural at negotiating, he doesn't realize how hard it is for other people. He discounts a skill that comes so easily to him.

But the big reason, I think, is that he has been doing this successfully for so long that he doesn't want to be taken out of the game. Losing the client would be a blow to his and our corporate image as experts in this field. Thus, when a consulting client pushes him on our fee (which is their negotiating right), he doesn't work as hard to maintain it. He yields because he wants to stay in the game. He will convince himself that any fee is worth it if it keeps us in that consulting role. We'll make up the loss by all the new clients our visibility attracts.

It took me a few years to appreciate how this executive's desire to stay in the game was costing our company money. Even though he was out in the marketplace negotiating ever-larger deals for our clients, the steadily reduced fees were making the activity ever less profitable. My solution: When it comes to negotiating *for* the client, I let him handle it. When it comes to negotiating *with* the client, though, I send along a couple of his colleagues who have had similar success in this line of work. They're not emotionally wedded to the client. They don't need to stay in the game at all costs. They still think big.

If they can fill up the room with examples of the big numbers they've generated in other parts of the world, they are perfect protection. With big numbers surrounding the discussion, it's much harder for the client to bring up small numbers and even harder for this executive to accept it.

Which brings us to the final point.

5. THEY ARE SURROUNDED BY SMALL NUMBERS.

Surrounding yourself with small numbers is the biggest obstacle to thinking big. You can't suddenly start negotiating multimillion-dollar contracts if all you've ever done are $10,000 contracts. You may have the skills. You may be asking a fair price. The other side may even agree that it's a fair price. The only problem is the other side is not prepared to accept that big number from you.

To think big in a negotiation today you have to prove that you have thought big in the past. You can do that by hinting at the kind of numbers your product or service has generated on other occasions. If you litter the discussion with big numbers (genuine, not inflated), eventually the other side will be acclimated to hearing them from you. It's a subtle tactic, but sometimes the other side will give you the opening to employ it.

I recall having lunch with the boss of a small but growing company. He was interested in using one of our older athletes as his spokesperson. The lunch was not to sell him on the athlete—he definitely wanted him. The only unresolved issue was price.

As you can imagine, the price of an athlete endorsement is flexible. Athletes don't have a "suggested retail price" stuck on their foreheads for sponsors. The price is a function of many variables—e.g., what the athlete is expected to do, the incremental sales he or she generates, the size and wealth of the sponsor, how much the athlete likes the company's products. In this case, the athlete was in the mature phase of his career. His best years were behind him. On the other hand, he was a proven winner with a terrific image. He might not be worth what he was at his peak, but he was valuable.

I had a mininum number of $100,000 a year, below which we wouldn't have a deal. There are some negotiations when it pays to be up front about the price. You take your minimum, mark it up 100 percent, and start negotiating there. But I didn't have a clue how big the company's boss was thinking. I wasn't sure how well his company was doing or what he could afford. It was possible that he was willing to pay much more than the minimum. The purpose of the lunch was to find out.

The first hour was a cat-and-mouse game. He described how he wanted to make the athlete the cornerstone of his marketing campaign. But he was careful not to make himself sound too rich. "We're a private company," he kept saying. "It's just me and my son." He was skirting the price issue, and

I was determined not to quote the first number. I didn't want to start too low.

As dessert came, I still didn't know what price range this fellow was in—until he asked what other sponsors had done in the past. This was my opening, my big chance to run through this aging athlete's impressive endorsement history. I told him about the $750,000-a-year contract six years earlier, the $500,000 contract in Japan, and so on. As I surrounded our discussion with hefty six-figure sums, I could see he was impressed but not scared away.

In effect, he was letting me think big. When I asked for $300,000 a year, he accepted on the spot without flinching. With all those other large figures still floating in the air, it probably seemed like a reasonable price.

START HIGH OR START LOW, BUT DON'T START IN BETWEEN

As anyone will tell you, the key to successful investing is "buy low, sell high." This is the wisest, most enduring, most profound statement ever made about investing. It is also the most meaningless.

The trouble is no one really knows what high or low actually is. It keeps moving. You can study the standard data to determine if a stock is overpriced or a bargain, such as return on equity, cash flow, price/earnings ratio, and the like. But the moment you think a stock has hit rock bottom, it goes even lower. Likewise, the moment you think a stock has topped out, it goes even higher.

"Buy low, sell high" is different in negotiating. In a negotiation, people actually come out and tell you what high or low is. If they're selling, the high mark is the first price they quote. If they're buying, rock bottom is their opening bid.

Let's say you're buying a house. You find one in an upper-middle-class community where housing prices are stable. The owners have lived there 14 years, during which time they've spent considerable sums on improvements and general maintenance. The house is in immaculate, move-in condition. The asking price is $795,000.

I realize this is a lot more than most people pay for a home. But for the purpose of discussing negotiating strategy, $795,000 is an interesting price point. It means you're buying more than a bare-bones form of shelter. You're looking for something "special," and special features tend to be pricey but extremely negotiable. Hard-to-quantify factors such as location, architectural details, landscaping, the quality of neighboring homes—what those in real estate call "curb appeal"—may be inflating the price. You can also be sure that the owners paid far less than $795,000 when they bought the house 14 years ago. In other words, there may be a lot of room to negotiate in that list price. (It's the difference between negotiating with an auto dealer for an $8,900 Ford Escort or an $89,000 Mercedes; the dealer has a lot more price flexibility and more room to give with the high-priced Mercedes.)

If you're buying a home, you face a lot of uncertainties. But there's one thing you can be sure of: If you pay the $795,000 asking price, you are definitely not "buying low." Unless the seller is a fool or desperate to sell, you can be sure that price point is the absolute top. The seller who gets that figure is definitely "selling high."

The reality of the negotiating dynamics of home buying is this: All sellers are prepared to take less than the asking price, and all buyers know that. It's interesting to see what buyers do with that information. They know the seller is making a high demand but is willing to take less. Yet they don't act as aggressively as they should on that knowledge. Instead of treating that $795,000 asking price with the disdain it deserves, they dignify it. They use it as the starting point for their opening bid.

We all know this mating dance. The buyer subtracts the standard 10 percent from the list price (i.e., $80,000) and offers $715,000 for the house. The seller naturally refuses this first bid, but agrees to lower the price by, say, $15,000. The buyer, in turn, increases his or her offer by an equal sum. Everyone knows where this routine is headed. After two or three offers and counteroffers, the two sides inevitably split the difference at $755,000. The buyer has increased his or her offer by $40,000. The seller has sacrificed an equivalent sum. In effect, by discounting the seller's inflated price by the "standard" 10 percent and splitting the difference, the buyer has ensured that he or she will get a less-than-standard result—in this case, a house at only 5 percent off.

The buyer could do infinitely better by remembering two immutable laws of negotiating:

•**Sellers do better when they make high demands.**

•**Buyers do better when they make low offers.**

The two are not mutually exclusive. It's not enough to realize that the seller is starting high. As a buyer, you have to be willing to start low—and not just low, but "insultingly" low.

138

If I were bidding on that $795,000 house, my opening offer would be at least 20 to 30 percent lower—say, $575,000.

The seller might scoff at the offer, which I could always increase. (Anyone can stay in the game if he or she is constantly willing to pay more.)

The seller might counter with a slightly lower price, initiating a split-the-difference scenario that ends up at $685,000. (That's certainly an improvement on an opening bid of $715,000 that ends up at $755,000.)

But I will never learn how much room to negotiate the other side has unless I give myself as much room as possible. Starting very low is the best way to do that.

THE "INSULTING" OFFER IS NOT INSULTING

I'm not sure why people are reluctant to make an insultingly low offer or even why they think lowballing is "insulting." Perhaps they don't want to appear as if they can't afford something. Perhaps they put too much faith in the "suggested retail price." Perhaps they're ignorant or haven't done their homework and they don't know what a "fair price" actually is.

I see variations on these themes inside our company, even when it's obvious that we are holding all the cards in a negotiation.

Some years ago, when the division chief of one of our major corporate customers suddenly found himself out of a job, there was a movement among several of our senior executives to hire this man. They had done a lot of business with him over the years and liked him.

I asked the executive leading the charge for this man's hiring what exactly he would do at our company, since his skills overlapped with a few people already on board. He said, "He's talented, he's got great industry contacts, and he's available. He'll make something happen."

Then I asked what it would cost us to hire him. He told me his annual compensation package at his old job added up to $250,000 (an extremely generous sum back then, which partially explained why he was out of work) but suggested that we could get him for $200,000.

This flabbergasted me—not just because $200,000 was excessive (it was!) but because of the frighteningly unsound negotiating logic our executive employed to get to that figure.

Our executive was so focused on the hefty compensation his friend was accustomed to that he regarded it as the starting point of any salary negotiation we might have with him. In his mind, we might not have to match the salary to land this fellow, but we would have to come close. In effect, he was ceding the high ground to his friend. He was allowing him to start high.

I didn't see it that way.

For one thing, he was out of work. There's a difference between "He earned $250,000" and "He's earning $250,000 now." I might have to subsidize the latter, but not the former.

Second, we didn't really need to hire him. He was available and might add some depth to our executive ranks, but we would survive without him. He was "nice to have" not "must have" executive talent.

Third, no one could tell me exactly what he was bringing to the party. If he came to us on day one with two or three clients in his pocket, each representing solid, determinable income, I could see paying him whatever he wanted. He would be worth it. Absent that, however, he was all investment and no foreseeable return, all risk and no reward.

I also thought that our company deserved a "premium" simply for being who we are. I don't delude myself that we're an industrial giant like General Motors or a marketing powerhouse like Procter & Gamble, but in our little segment of the sports business, we've always had a world-class reputation. We're the market leader. Landing at our company might appeal to him as a step up, a move to a better neighborhood. I didn't quite feel that he should be paying us for the privilege of working at our company, but I thought our reputation should count for something.

In my mind, all these factors dramatically strengthened our negotiating posture and virtually canceled out any right this fellow had to use his previous paycheck as the dollar anchor for a salary demand.

When I instructed our people to make him a very low offer, they thought he would be insulted. When he eventually signed on with us at one-third of his previous compensation, they were surprised. I was not.

THE FIRST NUMBER IS THE MOST DANGEROUS

A skilled negotiator knows that the most dangerous number in any negotiation is the first dollar figure mentioned. This is the "dollar anchor," the high or low number that frames the entire discussion that follows. It's dangerous because unless you're the one quoting the number, you can never be sure if it's legitimate or bogus, fair or excessive. You don't know where it came from or who made it up.

As a negotiator, I treat every first number with extreme skepticism. If I'm buying, I assume the other side is starting high with their asking price. If I'm selling, I assume the other side is starting low. And I respond in the extreme. If the other side is asking $100 and I'm prepared to pay $60, I don't offer $60 or, for that matter, $50. I start at $30 or perhaps $20. By increasing the distance between the other side and me, I've increased the amount of room I have to move up on price. At the same time I've increased the room the other side has to move down.

Start low or start high, but unless you enjoy cramped, confining spaces that reduce your options and limit your room to maneuver, don't start in between.

BEWARE THE BUBBLE EFFECT

To the untrained eye, our company appears to have two structural advantages that give us the license to think big.

(1) We negotiate for clients, not for ourselves. This is the "If you represent yourself, you have a fool for a client" theory. It's allegedly easier to be an aggressive advocate for another party than for yourself.

(2) Our clients tend to be superstars, gold medalists, and world champions. How tough can it be to negotiate a big deal for someone who is the biggest deal in his or her field?

The reality is a little more complicated.

Yes, it's nice to negotiate for an absent party if only because being able to say "I'll have to check with my client" is one of the great (and underrated) negotiating tools. The dark side of all this, of course, is that you do have to check with the client, and clients don't always give you the answer you want to hear.

For example, ever since Andre Agassi won Wimbledon in 1992, the experts in our London literary division have been saying that they could negotiate huge publishing contracts (books, calendars, newspaper columns, etc.) for Agassi. But Andre, for perfectly legitimate reasons, is not interested in writing his life story. He's still young. He likes his privacy. He'd rather focus on tennis than take time out to produce a book. So he says no to any publishing offers. That's the dark side of negotiating for clients. No matter how brilliantly you maneuver on their behalf, they have the right to say, "No, thank you."

It gets darker when the client is a superstar. Yes, representing top-tier clients improves our access, credibility, and authority to think big. But it also raises the financial hurdles we have to clear. A $100,000 endorsement contract that would thrill a middle-tier player in golf or tennis would be unremarkable to a top-tier player. At some point, in some sports, superstars achieve a threshold where they don't need more money.

Superstars don't just set the bar higher. They *keep* raising it, no matter what you do. Superstars have egos. They often have an inflated sense of their worth. They're very competitive. They hear what their rivals are making (which isn't always true). It isn't enough that the deal you negotiate for them is fair, elegant, and rich. It has to be richer than anyone else's.

I don't mention this to elicit sympathy. Believe me, I'd rather have world-class clients (with all their demands) than not have them. But it points up a pernicious dynamic that deludes people into thinking big when they really should be thinking about other things.

Considering the bubble that many highly paid athletes live in these days, surrounded by supporters, admirers, and hangers-on constantly telling them how great they are, it's easy to see how athletes get in the habit of thinking big about themselves. This is the "bubble effect," the delusion of grandeur that comes from analyzing your position and measuring your worth by talking only to people who agree with you or have the same vested interest.

I see this bubble effect in all sorts of negotiations, even salary reviews. If I ask an employee what kind of increase would make him or her happy, most of the time the employee responds with a number that's incredibly close to the one I had in mind. That makes sense. If you ask good people what would be fair, they'll usually be fair-minded.

But there are always people who take my request as a license to shoot for the moon. They quote a figure that's totally out of line with their achievements and what their peers are making. If I scratch below the surface, I usually find evidence of the bubble effect. Sometimes it's a spouse egging them on, saying, "The company doesn't appreciate you!" Or a close friend whispering in their ear about how much their counterparts at other companies are earning. Or it's simply a case of an employee talking to him- or herself, reviewing all the plusses and conveniently ignoring the minuses, slowly stoking him- or herself up into a bolder, more outlandish position.

The specifics vary, but the root cause is always the same. This type of employee is shut off in an insular environment where all he hears are his friends, well-wishers, and himself.

Dissenting voices from the outside are not invited. With the chorus of agreement ringing in their ears and inspiring them to new heights, it's not surprising that employees think big—bigger than they might deserve.

As the boss, it's my job to bring them back to earth. But I'd be much more impressed (and generous) if they had done it on their own—by seeking advice outside their cozy bubble.

The bubble effect is most dangerous in competitive bidding situations. After all, there's no advantage to thinking big if another bidder wins out by thinking a little less big.

We saw the bubble effect at work last year negotiating on behalf of the Orange Bowl. The Orange Bowl is a football stadium in Miami, Florida, that for over 60 years has hosted a New Year's Day game between two of America's best college football teams.

Collegiate sports are strictly amateur in the United States, but they are big business. Football is the biggest sport of all. Yet unlike every other collegiate sport—from basketball to swimming to field hockey—college football has no tournament or play-off system to determine that year's national champion. There is no season-ending championship game between the two teams with the best records. Instead, the various regional champions play each other in six bowl games on New Year's Day: the Rose Bowl in Pasadena, California; the Sugar Bowl in New Orleans, Louisiana; the Cotton Bowl in Dallas, Texas; the Fiesta Bowl in Tempe, Arizona; the Gator Bowl in Jacksonville, Florida; and the Orange Bowl. At day's end, a hundred or so football coaches and journalists assess the games and vote on which team should be the national champion.

It may be a curious system, but it has thrived for years because each bowl game is a financial success in its local market. The system's only drawback is the occasional controversy in determining a definitive national champion.

In 1994 there was an attempt to solve the problem. All of the regional conferences (except for the two that were contracted to the Rose Bowl) agreed to form an entity called the Alliance, which would guarantee that for the next six years the two best teams in the country would meet on New Year's Day in one of three rotating bowl games. The Alliance invited the various bowl games to submit blind bids to determine which three would share this "championship" game every third year.

Our client was the Orange Bowl. We had already completed two major assignments for the Orange Bowl. We had sold the Orange Bowl broadcast rights to CBS for $86 million over six years and secured a six-year $26 million sponsorship agreement with Federal Express.

Our new assignment was to advise the Orange Bowl on the size of its bid to be part of the Alliance. This is where the bubble effect kicked in.

Given the television and sponsorship revenues involved, we knew the bidding would start at $100 million. But as we huddled with the client, the discussion always veered to the inherent superiority of the Orange Bowl.

It had terrific location. Miami is a booming cosmopolitan city with sufficient attractions for corporate entertaining.

It had sunny weather in January and beautiful beaches, which appealed to the football coaches who regarded Miami as a nice vacation/reward for the players.

Most important, it had the tradition and image as the premier bowl game. Through luck, pluck, and sheer showmanship, the Orange Bowl had consistently attracted the best teams. Since the 1970s, the mythical national championship was played out more often in the Orange Bowl than any other bowl game.

In other words, the Orange Bowl Committee thought it had the best product. As their adviser, we were inclined to agree with them. (That's why we liked them as a client. They were the best.) As we prepared our bid, the belief that the Orange Bowl was "first among equals" took hold and infected our thinking.

The situation was already precarious. If our bid was too high, the Orange Bowl would lose money and its financial viability. If the bid was too low, the Orange Bowl would be shut out of the championship game. It would lose its top-shelf status. The CBS television deal would have to be renegotiated. The sponsor would be unhappy. It was quite likely that the Orange Bowl would go out of business. At IMG, we did not want to be known as the negotiators who killed the Orange Bowl.

But that didn't stop us from thinking big. Holed up with our client, we were convinced we deserved a premium for having the best product. We shaved a few million dollars from our bid (minimizing your cost is thinking big, too). Our one-shot bid of $102 million turned out to be considerably less than the $110 to $115 million bids submitted by the Gator, Fiesta, and Sugar bowls. Our bid was fourth! We had achieved the unthinkable: Our client was potentially shut out of the championship.

In hindsight, our mistake was falling prey to the bubble effect. We were so swept up by the Orange Bowl's established prestige that we forgot that our job was to tell the Orange Bowl Committee that maybe it wasn't in their best negotiating interest to consider themselves more equal than the competition. In a competitive situation, thinking you're the best could be a disadvantage.

We also didn't look at the situation from the Alliance commissioners' viewpoint (always a big mistake). We thought the Orange Bowl's advantages were self-evident. How could the commissioners ignore them? We forgot that it wasn't their job to favor our client. Their job was to be impartial and fair. That's what a blind bidding format ensures.

I probably wouldn't be forthcoming with this incident if it didn't contain a happy ending. After some serious repositioning, we were able to convince the commissioners that the Orange Bowl's nonfinancial factors—its venue, weather, and tradition—counted for something. With a little sweetening, they accepted our bid.

But I hate to think how close we came to disaster. That's the danger of thinking big in a closed room. When you talk only to yourself, you can talk yourself into a disaster.

● ● ●

THE McCORMACK RULES

- There is an unspoken caste system in any organization based on whether you think big or small or somewhere in between.

- Doing bigger deals is a matter of attitude. It's a matter of knowing and believing that your product or service is worth it and then overcoming all the mental blocks that force you to think small.

- There's a difference between negotiating for someone else and for yourself. It's easier to argue that someone else's product is "the best in the world" and worth top dollar than it is to say it about yourself. The former is advocacy, the latter braggadocio.

- Surrounding yourself with small numbers is the biggest obstacle to thinking big. You can't suddenly start negotiating multimillion-dollar contracts if all you've ever done are $10,000 contracts.

- Sellers do better when they make high demands. Buyers do better when they make low offers.

- The most dangerous number in any negotiation is the first dollar figure mentioned. Treat it with extreme skepticism.

- Start low or start high, but unless you enjoy cramped, confining spaces that reduce your options and limit your room to maneuver, don't start in between.

- The dark side of negotiating for other people is that no matter how brilliantly you maneuver on their behalf, they always have the right to say, "No, thank you."

- When you talk only to yourself, you can talk yourself into disasters.

CHAPTER 6

Advanced Techniques to Advance Your Side of the Bargain

HOW TO BREAK AN IMPASSE

I wonder how many deals a day in any company never happen because the seller and buyer have reached a negotiating impasse—and don't know how to break it. I wonder how much business is lost because, with positions entrenched and egos locked in place, the combatants aren't clever enough to find a face-saving tactic that will get them moving toward each other again. I suspect the number of lost deals would frighten most bosses.

Walking away from an impasse is not all bad, of course.

I used to believe that if people wanted a transaction to happen, it would happen. If a deadlock arose, it was all right to yield because getting the deal done was more important than getting the deal done correctly. I don't believe or endorse that anymore. A bad deal always leaves one party unsatisfied. Sooner or later, that party will find a way to get out of it. In that sense, it's better to walk away from an impasse than to resolve it in the other side's favor.

I also think that the massive cost-containment pressures at most companies have made people more jittery about resolving impasses. People don't want to look as if they're overpaid or sold too cheaply. With all the downsizings, demands for multiple bids, and easy access to information, people are more self-conscious that someone somewhere will question their deal-making prowess. So they'll walk rather than try harder.

It doesn't have to be that way. Depending on the circumstances, breaking an impasse has nothing to do with paying more or accepting less. It has everything to do with creating a slight shift in the negotiating terrain. Here are four simple tactics to break an impasse.

1. DON'T SWEAT THE DETAILS.

If I have a managerial or negotiating weakness, it's that I tend to treat most dilemmas with a broad brush. I don't have the time or desire to stick my hands into the murky details of most transactions. I did the detail work when I was a young attorney, poring over contracts. I did the same when I began managing golfers (who else would do it?). Nowadays, I can delegate the details, and I do it without thinking.

That automatic urge to brush aside problematic details is a great negotiating tool. As a manager, I've resolved many internal squabbles by bringing the two combatants together, listening to their differences, and more or less ignoring the differences. I tell them, "Why don't the two of you put aside your petty grievances and start working together? Then let's meet again in a month and see if you still feel the same way." More often than not, if you force people to function as allies, they quickly forget their designated roles as adversaries.

It's no different in a deadlocked deal. With broad brush in hand, I will often tell the other side, "Look, we're not going to resolve these issues now. We agree on the fundamentals. Why don't we get started working together and agree that the unresolved issues will be negotiated in good faith later?" My negotiating motto is "Let's get started!" because I know once the other side and I become allies, we are less likely to think like adversaries.

2. CHANGE THE PLAYERS.

Sometimes impasses arise because of bad personal chemistry. It's not the deal terms that stall the negotiation; it's the dealer who's demanding them. The two sides don't like each other anymore.

The simple solution would be to substitute a more appropriate player. It's certainly that simple in sports. If a baseball pitcher is getting pounded by the other side, the manager brings in a new pitcher, usually one who throws from the opposite side of the mound and who has a slightly different array of pitches.

It's not that simple in business. There seems to be an unwritten code that the people who initiated the deal are the ones who close the deal. They get to stay in the game even if they are no longer effective.

My advice to any negotiator is: Question the code. If you can't get the job done, take yourself out of the game. Put in someone who can. The other side won't think less of you for it. If they really want the deal to go through, they'll probably be grateful.

3. BRING IN IMPLEMENTERS.

Most negotiators tend to be extremely competitive. That's what makes them valuable. They're willing to scratch and claw for the deal points that others leave behind. But that attitude is not always appropriate.

In my mind, an impasse is often a signal that the negotiation needs to move from a competitive mode to a cooperative mode. Hence, you need to inject a different sort of person into the discussion, someone who isn't in the room to argue but rather to cooperate.

A few years ago I was involved in a protracted negotiation for the sponsorship of a sporting event. We were negotiating a long-term deal, with escalating payments from the sponsor each year. We hit a snag over the size of the yearly increases, in large part because we understood how much more valuable the event would be three or five years down the road and the sponsor didn't. It was a serious impasse.

As a change of pace at one session, I invited one of our senior television technicians to talk about the incredible changes brewing in broadcast and satellite technology and the growth of television's reach in various parts of the world. I intended it as a mild distraction. I wasn't prepared for how impressive the technical presentation would be or how much it would impress the sponsor. But it did. Within the span of that session, the sponsor began to understand the true value of the event and accepted our escalating fee structure.

As a negotiator, I didn't have the knowledge or authority to make those claims for the event. As the fellow actually implementing the broadcast of the event, our technical executive did.

If you reach an impasse because the other side doesn't believe all the claims you are making for your product or service, don't blame them for being skeptical. Bring in an implementer who has the expertise and credibility to make those claims stick.

4. TELL A JOKE.

A well-timed wisecrack can puncture the tensions and pretensions of any impasse. But you have to be bold, blunt, and quick to pull it off.

My friend Ben Bidwell is one of the sharpest wits I know, and he has used his blunt tongue often to wrench himself out of stalemates. In the early 1970s, when Bidwell was running Ford's Lincoln-Mercury division, the bean counters at headquarters concluded that the Mercury Cougar was a financial drain on the division. It ought to be killed. Bidwell thought this was ludicrous, not the least because a cougar was Mercury's advertising symbol and slogan ("The Sign of the Cat").

A meeting was called by Henry Ford II to decide the Mercury Cougar's fate. Ford went around the room, polling the executives, who with rare unanimity agreed that the Cougar must go. Bidwell didn't say a word. Commenting on

Bidwell's silence, Henry Ford said, "We haven't heard from you yet, Bidwell. What do you think?"

Bidwell paused and said, "I have just one thing to say, Mr. Ford. You can't run a cathouse without a cat."

It took a moment for the quip to sink in. Then Henry Ford started to laugh, and the rest of the room joined in. One joke. One stalemate averted.

It Takes Three to Play Hardball

Playing hardball in business means taking a difficult stand on a certain position—and, more important, standing by it.

It's the moment when you throw out all the textbook rules about "win-win" negotiating and stake out precisely for the other party how much you expect to win, regardless of how much the other side claims they might lose.

The majority of people tend to be clumsy at hardball. They're impatient. They misread the other side. They miscalculate their leverage. They don't have a long-term goal underlying their obstinacy.

You see this most often in people who think playing hardball means being tough or aggressive in one-on-one situations. On the contrary, I don't think you can play hardball one-on-one—because at any point the other side can simply refuse to play and walk away from the table.

To effectively play hardball in business you always need an influential third party that keeps everyone at the table. Without that third party influencing the situation, you're not playing hardball, you're just making it hard to get things done.

In most businesses, the third party can be a demanding boss who wants the transaction completed. It can be a clock ticking toward a deadline, forcing you to get something done. In a court of law, where attorneys play hardball often and well, the third party is usually a judge or jury. In our business, it is often the hue and cry of the general public.

Our negotiation in Hong Kong in the late 1980s on behalf of Wimbledon with TVB, one of the most profitable television networks in the world, illustrates my point. It involved the sale of television rights to the Wimbledon finals in Hong Kong.

We do extensive research about what TV networks pay for sporting events. Consequently, we have a good idea of the relative value of most events in most markets.

We concluded that TVB was paying nowhere near enough for the Wimbledon rights. TVB had been gently escalating their payments by two or three thousand dollars each year, which we felt was underpricing the world's most prestigious tennis tournament.

So we decided to make an issue of this in Hong Kong. We asked TVB for a significant increase. They countered with an unacceptable offer, contending that showing the Wimbledon finals live in Hong Kong was not that big a deal to the general public. "Nobody really cares," they said.

We didn't agree. "If it's not a big deal," we said, "why don't you broadcast delayed coverage at this price?" Having said it wasn't a big deal, they had to agree.

We also invited them to help us put together a live closed-circuit telecast of Wimbledon for the few Hong Hong tennis enthusiasts who cared. They liked that idea, and we proceeded along that track.

Then the influential third party appeared. When the press learned that there would be no live coverage of Wimbledon, there was an enormous public outcry.

TVB backed off their agreement to help us with the live closed-circuit telecast. Instead they told the Hong Kong press that we had forced them to take the delayed broadcast and that our ulterior motive was to milk the Hong Kong public for more money and turn Wimbledon into an event for the elite rather than the people. TVB went even further by threatening to stop us from getting our license to show the closed-circuit telecast—which, given their connections, they could easily do.

I suppose this strategy of taking their case to the people was hardball, but it wasn't very effective.

After all, we still controlled the one ingredient the Hong Kong public was clamoring for, namely the live broadcast of Wimbledon.

And so we began to play hardball. We told TVB that we were prepared to keep Wimbledon off the air entirely in Hong Kong unless they came up with a significant increase in rights payments.

Because the uproar was so great, TVB at the last minute backed down. In the end, we doubled the rights fees for our client.

The hardball element in all this was our willingness to pull Wimbledon off the air. But I don't think we would have succeeded—or even tried—without the Hong Kong public behind us.

The next time you put yourself on the line in a negotiation—whether you're asking for a raise, challenging a superior, or closing a big deal—ask yourself these two questions: Is there an influential third party interested in how this duel turns out? And is that third party on my side?

So, the Other Side Is Making Last-Minute Changes?

In negotiating, few tactics are as irritating as a counterpart who seeks to change the terms of the deal at the last minute. It poses the dilemma: Is it better to walk away or cave in?

Before you do either, ask yourself: Are these people sneaky? Are 11th-hour demands their standard operating procedure? If so, walk away.

Or are they victims of circumstances beyond their control? Most people don't go through the trouble of altering an agreement at the last minute because they want to, but rather because they have to.

We see this with surprising frequency in the sports sponsorship business. The commercial side of a sporting event involves so many competing elements—athletes, promoters, sponsors, concessions, television—that conflicts about who is entitled to what are almost inevitable. At some point, someone is going to think they bought the rights to something from someone who may or may not control those rights.

Let me give you a minor but typical example. One of our corporate clients sponsored a bowling tournament in the midwest. For a substantial sum of money, our client was allowed to name the event after one of their products, hang banners at the site promoting that product, and most important, advertise the product on the two pin sweeps (the arms that drop down and clear the fallen pins after each ball) during the tournament finals, which would be televised on a sports network.

The pin sweeps were the heart of the deal. In bowling, a TV camera can ignore the banners and signs hanging throughout the venue, but it cannot avoid the pins being knocked down and the pin sweeps clearing them. The sponsor's image would appear on TV every time a ball was thrown—and then again with the slow-motion replay! In marketing, these product "impressions" are very important.

The day of the finals, the event organizer informed us that the sponsor was entitled to advertise on only one of the two pin sweeps. This was bad news for two reasons: Not only was our client receiving only half the benefit he thought he was buying, but time was running out.

The normal response in this situation is to turn confrontational. When somebody burns you, you want to burn them back. You rant and rave, call them names, threaten to go to their superiors or take them to court. But this would not have solved the immediate problem of getting our client's name on both pin sweeps.

Instead, our people at the event calmly analyzed the situation and concluded that the event organizer wasn't being sneaky or malicious. He was being pressured by the television network, which thought it was entitled to put its own message on one of the pin sweeps.

We didn't take offense at this last-minute disturbance. In fact, we stayed out of it completely. As far as we were concerned, the organizer had a problem with the television network, not with us. Our client had paid for two pin sweeps—and we would accept nothing less. If the organizer couldn't deliver them, then we would renegotiate our fee after the event, when we could more accurately assess the impact of the change.

Faced with the prospect of a drastically reduced fee (which he, no doubt, had already mentally banked) for a perishable product (the pin sweeps would be worthless the next day), the organizer quickly gave us the second pin sweep.

In my experience, the best way to disarm someone who puts a gun to your head is to act as if the gun isn't loaded.

HOW TO SAY YES, NO, OR MAYBE—AND MEAN IT

In any negotiation, there are three responses when the other side makes an offer. You can accept it, reject it, or ask them to try again.

Accepting someone's offer should be the simplest and most gratifying gesture in business. You've closed a sale. You say yes, shake hands, and proceed with the transaction.

Yet people manage to get even this wrong. The biggest sin: They get greedy. They have second thoughts about the price, thinking they could have gotten more. If they act on these doubts, the results can be disastrous.

1. SAY YES WITHOUT SECOND THOUGHTS.

I remember a few years ago when a woman I respect was negotiating to buy a media property. The sellers had shopped the property around for several months and concluded that this woman was the only seriously interested buyer. She was aware of this and opened the negotiation with a lowball bid of $3.5 million.

The sellers, not unexpectedly, responded that they had a larger sum in mind. Citing recent sales of similar properties and the industry's standard multiple of earnings, they countered in writing that a more acceptable figure would be somewhere between $6.5 million and $8 million. The woman took them at their word and made a final offer of $7 million—which, given the fact that she was the only interested buyer, would have been a real coup for the sellers.

But they were graceless in accepting her offer. Rather than simply saying yes and appreciating the fact that she had literally doubled her offer and more than met their acceptable minimum, the sellers tried to bump her up several hundred thousand dollars closer to $8 million.

The woman ended the negotiation immediately. She withdrew her $7 million offer and, for good measure, her $3.5 million offer. She refused to entertain the seller's pleas to reopen the discussions—which, given the circumstances, was the appropriate response. The property has yet to be sold.

As a general rule of salesmanship, if the buyer meets or exceeds your price and you have the nagging feeling that you can get a little more, keep the secret to yourself.

2. SAY NO WITHOUT INSULTING.

Rejecting an offer, theoretically, should be even simpler than saying yes. You say no and walk away, hopefully as friends who will do business again in the future. But again, many people get it wrong. They just can't say no and leave it at that. They have to cite reasons.

The trouble with explaining a rejection is that, by definition, it will rarely sound positive.

In our business, for example, there have been times when an athlete client has had to choose between competing offers from, say, four sports apparel companies. In many cases, money is not the issue. The client prefers one manufacturer's style, reputation, or advertising strategy over the others' and is willing to take less money to be associated with what is perceived as a classier line.

We have to be very careful how we say no to the losing bidders (with whom we presumably want to do business again on behalf of other clients). The last thing they need to hear from us is that client x thought their designs were ugly or their advertising was silly. We simply say no—without insulting them.

3. SAY MAYBE AND BE PATIENT.

The most important rejection in a negotiation, of course, is the one that keeps the door slightly open—the "maybe" that really means "no."

When the other side makes an unacceptable offer, avoid the instant reaction. A quick "no" is usually emotional and invariably sounds dismissive, as if the other side has insulted your intelligence. It creates a personal gap that dollar figures often can't bridge. You never know how the other side will react.

We were recently selling a publishing project to a company that we had successfully dealt with many times before. The only issue on the table was price.

The company's president, whom I knew to be a strong-willed and sometimes inflexible negotiator, opened with a nice round number—which was about a third of what I expected.

I said nothing. I let the number hang there between us, refusing to touch it. My goal: Don't be confrontational. I figured that the president was a volatile person who might react badly to my dismissing his offer. I didn't want him angrily cutting me off and saying, "Well, then, let's forget it. . . ."

Instead, I began to talk about the nonmonetary points of the project. I expressed enthusiasm about his staff and the fact that we would be working together again. I asked to hear more about their marketing plans and how they expected to make money off the project.

The president took the bait. He was very proud of his organization and their ability to create winners. In effect, he began to sell to me. As he proceeded to boast about the great job his people could do, I was recalibrating my asking price—upward.

TURNING CONCESSIONS INTO VICTORIES

Although no two negotiations are ever exactly alike, they all have one thing in common: At some point, you will be expected to make a concession.

There's nothing wrong with that. Negotiation is, after all, give and take. Giving in is part of the drill.

Unfortunately, a lot of people have a problem with that. They regard any concession as an admission of weakness or failure, as if yielding on one point obliges them to yield on every point thereafter. And so they stubbornly refuse to yield on anything. We've seen negotiations fall apart even before they started because neither side was willing to concede on where the negotiations would take place or who would attend. Both sides equated concession with defeat.

I tend to go to the other extreme. I equate concession with winning. I never go into a negotiation without knowing exactly how much I am willing to concede. In my book, conceding a negotiating point is a golden opportunity to get something greater in return.

Basically, there are three ways to concede a point in a negotiation.

1. CONCEDE BUT GET NOTHING IN RETURN.

You'd be amazed at how many people negotiate this way—because it's so easy to do.

If the contractor renovating your house asks for a 30-day extension, do you let him off the hook? Or do you expect to be compensated for the concession? Do you ask for financial give-backs or invoke a lateness penalty?

Most people, I suspect, would let him off the hook. They want the contractor happy, not embittered, when he's working in their home, and they want him to finish the job. And they might have the feeling that he's holding a gun to their head. What choice do they have if he can't finish on time? And so they accommodate—because it's the path of least resistance.

On a scale of 1 to 10, I'd rate this type of concession a 5.

You've made the other side happy. But other than their goodwill, what have you got to show for it?

2. CONCEDE, BUT ONLY FOR SOMETHING OF EQUAL VALUE.

This is the tit-for-tat school of negotiating.

You want better payment terms? Place a bigger order.

You want a reduced price? Make a commitment today.

You want free shipping? Take delivery on Thursday.

Perfectly legitimate (and certainly an improvement on conceding for nothing), this concession rates an 8. You give an inch, you take an inch. The trouble is, you're never ahead of the game. Your position improves only as the other side's position improves. You're not really negotiating. You are running in place, only faster.

3. CONCEDE BUT GET MORE IN RETURN.

This concession is a perfect 10, especially if the other side doesn't know how little the concession costs you.

People often equate the value of a concession with how hard they had to work for it. If it takes them weeks of scrappy bargaining to win a price break from you, that concession somehow looms larger and more valuable than if you had given in on the spot. The net cost to you is the same either way, but the return is far greater if you make the other side squirm.

If you are alert, you can turn almost any negotiating point into a valuable concession.

The chairman of a European conglomerate a few years back was dissatisfied with the size of his company's hospitality tent at a major sporting event. He wanted a bigger tent and, since tents were limited, asked me if I could help out.

I told him that I would try my best, but I made it very clear that this would not be easy to orchestrate and that in return I expected some help on a television project being negotiated between our companies.

It turned out that it wasn't difficult to secure the larger tent. The event's directors thought the smaller tent was a fire hazard and quickly yielded to my request.

But I didn't tell the chairman that. I waited a few weeks, when all the arrangements were locked in, to bring him the good news. The chairman thought I had done a wonderful deal for him and that I had made a major effort on his behalf, and he was remarkably conciliatory in the television negotiation.

There's nothing particularly sly about this. As a negotiator, you are under no obligation to tell the other side that a concession is easy to make or immaterial to you. And you don't have to concede immediately.

In fact, conceding too quickly can paint you in a more unfavorable light than being difficult or intractable will. I would tend to suspect someone asking $100,000 for their product or service who, when I counter with a lowball offer of $50,000, accepts it on the spot (or even agrees to split the difference). While I might be glad that I got my price, I would always be wondering what other points in the deal were similarly inflated.

THE PARADOX OF SUCCESSFUL RELATIONSHIPS

In every business relationship, the parties involved start out thinking about the benefits they're getting from a deal and end up worrying more about the benefits the other side is getting from it.

This is certainly one of the more taxing aspects of our business, where we earn commissions during the life of any contract we negotiate. But it's an attitude, either out in the open or simmering below the surface, that probably exists in all partnerships and joint ventures. Some people always feel they're bringing more to the party than you are.

For example, say you are an athlete and I can conclude a contract that pays you $500,000 a year for endorsing a line of ashtrays. All you have to do is be available five days a year for meetings, photographs, and public appearances. An ashtray endorsement is such a remarkable deal that, initially, you will be glad to give me a 50 percent fee, double our usual commission. You'll congratulate me and say, "Where do I sign?"

But as you go into your ninth year of meetings and photo sessions and I'm still getting my 50 percent fee, your attitude will change. That's human nature (it wouldn't be any different if my fee were 5 percent). And I have to prepare for the day you realize that having your success means sharing it with me.

The paradox of long-term relationships is that to maintain them, you have to spend as much time protecting yourself from success as you do from failure.

Putting protective clauses in agreements and occasionally reminding a client or partner what you've done for him or her helps, but it's no guarantee that he or she won't forget.

Ideally, when you sign on to do a job for someone, you should be asking him or her, "Once I've built this for you, will you take it away?" If you are given verbal assurances, ask for them to be put in writing.

Unfortunately, this is the one contract point you frequently can't get. And even if you can, you're vulnerable at renewal time.

For example, consider this scenario: We approach a major American sporting event about selling its TV broadcast rights in a previously untapped market such as the United Kingdom. Since they have nothing to lose, the event's directors gladly give us our 25 percent commission. They even give us a three-year contract.

In year one, after working very hard to establish the event, we extract $100,000 for U.K. rights from the BBC. In year two, they pay $150,000. In year three, as the event catches on, the rights shoot up to $300,000.

You'd think everyone would be happy. But as year four approaches and our contract expires, the event's directors begin to change. They stop enjoying all the benefits they're getting from the deal—and start worrying about the benefits we're getting.

In their eyes, the potential revenues in year four are a windfall we had nothing to do with. Not only is the money higher than they ever imagined, but we don't have to work as hard to earn it! That's when they try to cut us down to 20 or 15 percent.

And that's when we have to decide if we can live with that—or walk.

Unfortunately, once the client starts slashing, it's hard to win the war of attrition if you don't have any leverage. A smart negotiator prepares for that day and makes sure the other side will feel some pain when the slashing begins.

Some years ago a classmate of mine found himself working as the exclusive distributor for an auto parts manufacturer in three midwestern states: Illinois, North Dakota, and South Dakota. It didn't take him long to start posting phenomenal sales in populous Illinois, particularly in the Chicago area. But he also had spent a lot of time driving around in sparsely populated North and South Dakota building up a promising customer base there.

The parent company was so impressed by his numbers that they congratulated him and told him they were taking Illinois off his hands. It was a big territory, they said, and they could serve it better with their own people. They didn't need an independent distributor anymore. This plan would cost my classmate 70 percent of his sales and nearly all of his profits. He was facing ruin, and it didn't look as if he had any valuable chips to bargain with.

His only strategy was to call their bluff. "If you like Illinois so much," he told them, "you can have the Dakota territories, too."

He reckoned the company was investing heavily to set up a sales network in the lucrative Illinois territory. It probably couldn't afford a similar investment in the lower-yielding Dakotas. He was right. Within a week the company changed its mind.

It's easier to make the other side feel your pain if you're involved in other parts of their business—that is, if they know you can cause a little pain too.

THE RIGHT TO SAY YES IS VERY VALUABLE

I've always placed a high premium on having the right to say yes in any negotiation. It means I have the final word. I control my own destiny. I can end the negotiation whenever I choose. I'm not hanging on every whim and word of the other fellow who has the right to say yes.

As a manager of my own company, I almost always have the final word in a discussion. After all, I'm running the company.

In a negotiation where I am a buyer of other people's products or services, I also retain the right to say yes. After all, the other side is importuning me to give them my money. They can't do a thing until I agree.

Unfortunately, in our business, I'm more often the seller in a negotiation. I'm the fellow importuning the other side to say yes.

As a result, I've become a connoisseur of openings in a negotiation where I can turn the tables on the other side and grab the right to say yes for myself. These openings don't appear that often, but they do seem to crop up in situations where one side is trying to shut out their competition. I've learned this the hard way, when other people have wrested yes from me.

A few years ago we licensed the rights to use a client's name on a sportswear line in the United Kingdom to a British manufacturer. The sale, which was conducted by a formal auction among several companies, generated a handsome guarantee against royalties. Our success in the U.K. market encouraged us to set up a similar auction in North America.

171

But we never got a chance. An American entrepreneur had somehow got ahold of our British proposal and fallen in love with the project. He called me up and said, in effect, "I want to sell this product line."

I said, "Well, we were going to submit it to several companies to gauge their level of interest."

"What kind of money are you looking at?" he asked.

"I have no idea, but given the bigger size of the U.S. market, we're hoping for at least four times the U.K. guarantee."

I thought this was a deft move. I knew he knew we had received £200,000 in the United Kingdom. By establishing the multiple of four, I had anchored our North American price tag at $1.2 million (the dollar equivalent of £800,000). If that didn't scare him off, he could certainly join in the auction. I was looking forward to seeing how much more we could generate when other bidders got involved.

But then he made an even more deft move. He said, "Mark, I really want this. Think of a number that's fair, and if I say yes, we have a deal."

With this one phrase, he accomplished several important negotiating objectives:

- By tempting me into a unilateral negotiation, he erased my right to shop the deal to other companies. He was shutting out his competition.

- By forcing *me* to make the offer, he was increasing his chances that I would underprice the project. He worked in the apparel business every day. I didn't. He had an insider's knowledge of what constituted a fair price and what was a bargain. Plus, if I quoted an outrageously high price, he could always say no.

- By grabbing the right to say yes away from me, he had dramatically foreshortened the negotiation. It wouldn't drag on for weeks. It would be over the moment he said yes or no.

For my part, I had good reasons to let him get away with this gambit. I knew the client would consider $1.2 million extremely generous. Also, I couldn't be sure we could match it in an auction. Plus, I was being given carte blanche to name my price. I've always thought that being able to say "You can have this for x dollars" is better than asking "What will you give me for this?" I gave up the right to say yes, but in exchange I got the right to name my price.

I gulped hard, tacked on an extra $50,000, and said, "The price is $1.25 million."

I could hear him sigh on the other end before he said, "Okay, we have a deal." But the sigh was pure acting, because he knew better than I that he had pulled off a negotiation. When you shut out the competition *and* get the other side to make the first offer, you have every right to feel you're getting a bargain.

AUCTIONS: NEGOTIATING'S HIGHEST LIFE-FORM

An auction is negotiating taken to its most sophisticated (and exciting) extreme. Not everyone can do it. Not only do you have to identify all the emotions and crosscurrents that lead normally sane people to overpay in an auction environment, but you have to know how to control these factors to your advantage. Making an auction pay off for you demands near-total mastery of all the major elements of good negotiating.

An auction forces you to *think big*. A lot of things can go wrong in an auction, but if you create the proper hothouse atmosphere, you will almost always be working at the top, not the bottom, of the price equation.

An auction forces you to *be prepared*. One-on-one negotiations are relatively simple. You find an interested party and start talking. Auctions force you to research the market for your product or service, find out who's interested, and get them into the bidding process.

Auctions force you to *question the rules*. By definition, an auction means you are not selling a commodity but rather something precious, rare, or one of a kind. There's no such thing as a standard auction. The ground rules change each time, depending on what's for sale, who's bidding, and why. The good news is that you get to write the rules, and your success is limited only by your creativity and willingness to challenge everyone's assumptions.

An auction demands *integrity* on your part. The combatants you invite to the party have to believe that you will stick to the ground rules, keep your word, and never favor one party over another.

An auction forces you to *deal with ambiguity and uncertainty*. The more bidders involved, the more ambiguity. Negotiating one-on-one is tough enough, like taming a lion in a cage. An auction is like trying to tame a string of lions. The circus atmosphere bewilders many people.

Most of all, though, an auction forces you to *deal with the many facets of competition*. A lot of people selling a product or service are good at negotiating one-on-one with a single buyer. But they're not as skilled at maximizing their position when two or more potential buyers are tossed into the negotiating mix.

I'm not sure why. In theory, when several parties are bidding against each other, it should be fairly easy to create a feeding frenzy that hikes up your price. I know that in our business when three or four teams compete to sign up a free-agent ballplayer, when several racquet manufacturers want to be associated with a superstar tennis player, or when three major television networks compete for the broadcast rights to a major sporting event, we usually get more than the market rate.

But even in this near-ideal negotiating situation, some people find a way to make less out of more. Quite often they're clumsy or sneaky in the way they expose the original party to the fact that other parties are interested.

Some years ago an up-and-coming golfer approached us about representing him. Over the course of a few weeks we devoted a lot of man-hours talking to him about a management relationship. We explained our fee structure and how we earned our commissions. We reviewed his contracts and finances, met with his family, analyzed his tournament schedule, and suggested some lucrative alternatives. We even floated his name to a few sponsors to gauge their interest in him. After a few weeks of this, he casually mentioned that he had also been talking to two of our competitors who—surprise!—were willing to reduce their commissions. Would we do the same?

I can't tell you how distasteful we found this approach— or how quickly we lost interest in him.

It wasn't because he was talking to other client managers. We could understand that. If an up-and-coming golfer wanted to be represented by our organization, I would tell him the best way to catch our attention (if we weren't already interested) would be to hint that our competition was seriously considering signing him—because our people will frequently go to great lengths to thwart the competition. (This plays on the axiom that an object is more desirable, and therefore more valuable, the moment someone else wants it too.)

But this fellow was clumsy in disclosing this point. He had led us to believe we were negotiating one-on-one in good faith, when in fact he was inviting us to join in a bidding war. The only hitch was he never sent us the invitation. He had used our interest to extract concessions from the competition and then came back to us to match them. If he had told us from the outset that other parties were interested, we might have admired his moxie. But withholding the information until the last moment suggested a sneakiness and lack of character that we would prefer to keep off our client roster. We were glad to let the competition "win" him.

I let this episode remind me how much ill will can be created by the clumsy introduction of competitors into a bidding war.

In our business, particularly at contract renewal time, bringing competition into the mix requires a delicate touch—because contract renewals mean the other side is an incumbent and incumbents have unique negotiating rights.

Let's say one of our athletes has a three-year endorsement deal with company x (the incumbent) that's up for renewal. As agents, it's our job to negotiate the best deal for the athlete. We can do this by letting other companies know the athlete is available and offering him or her up to the highest bidder. But this auction strategy isn't always possible or advisable.

For one thing, the incumbent has rights. There's usually some "exclusive negotiating period" or "right of first refusal" language in the contract that requires us to talk to company x first or lets x match any offer we get. That's a constraint on how openly we can talk to other parties.

The incumbent also knows the true value of their relationship with our client, simply by looking at his or her profit-and-loss statement. They also know the value of the deal's nonfinancial elements. Company representatives may simply like being friends with the athlete or having access to impossible-to-get tickets. If the original deal was a money maker or personally satisfying, it might be in our interest to negotiate unilaterally with the incumbent. Quite often a happy incumbent will pay a hefty premium simply to keep other bidders out.

Either way, as negotiators we've learned never to underestimate the importance of exclusivity to the other side.

Bringing second or third parties (the nonincumbents) into the negotiation is also not as simple as it looks. In sports, where we are often negotiating with a familiar handful of golf equipment manufacturers or tennis apparel companies or athletic-shoe makers or television networks, there is always the assumption that the nonincumbents are being used to drive up the price for the incumbent. Over the years I've noticed that the nonincumbents don't like playing the role of a stalking horse. It's not because they don't want to drive up their competition's costs. The real reason is more basic: *They don't like to lose.* They're competitive. They get caught up in the negotiation process, and they don't toss their hat into the ring to walk away empty-handed.

In an emotionally neutral world, this wouldn't matter. But the bidders in an auction are flesh-and-blood people. They have personal feelings, professional objectives, bosses to please, public profiles to protect, and self-images that need constant polishing. They are also our core customer base. We will have to deal with them again and again. They resent being lured into an auction process merely to be used as pawns in our chess game.

There have been occasions when outside parties have literally begged us to let them into a negotiation for the express purpose of making mischief for the incumbent. But as they begin to see all the benefits of the property we're selling, they get increasingly serious about their bid. They really want to win. We have to be very careful when our stalking horse turns into a legitimate thoroughbred. On the one hand, it's good for us because it raises the stakes. But it's tricky, too, because only one party will walk away happy. Everyone else will be disappointed. And we don't need the losers to blame us for that disappointment. (This is a real concern for us, so real that we have sometimes considered altering major deal points in a negotiation—such as changing the territory from the United Kingdom to the world or increasing the contract term from four years to five—to give the losing bidders a face-saving reason to walk away.)

CONSTRUCTING THE STATE-OF-THE-ART AUCTION

As I've said, auctions require a skill set that is beyond the grasp of the novice negotiator (and, in truth, many more experienced negotiators as well). The reality is most negotiations don't require those skills. Most negotiations are unilateral affairs, involving one buyer and one seller. I have a car. You want to buy it. If we can't strike a bargain, I'll find someone else willing to buy the car on my terms. You'll find someone else who is selling the same car. That's the negotiating equation most of us are familiar with.

Auctions, on the other hand, require a different set of circumstances. One, you need multiple bidders hungering for your product or service. Two, your product or service has to be rare, special, extremely limited in quantity (or disappearing quickly), or all of the above to attract multiple bidders. Three, you have to link these two factors. Rarity creates value. Rarity combined with value creates lust in the bidders.

Orchestrating this seemingly vicious circle of supply and demand makes an auction negotiating's highest life-form.

In one sense, you could make a strong argument that every good negotiator is constantly trying to artificially manufacture the favorable circumstances of an auction in situations where they are not present.

When the seller points out that inventory is low (whether it's true or not), he or she is trying to imbue the product with an aura of rarity.

When the seller hints that other parties have recently been to the office or toured the facility (again, whether true or not), the seller is trying to surround the negotiation with the specter of multiple bidders.

Likewise when the seller discloses what other parties have paid in the past, or suggests that the product may be discontinued or that prices may rise in the near future, or hauls out the time worn phrase "We've only got one left. I don't know when we'll get another shipment." All of these are tactics to contrive rarity or competition where none exists in order to capture a dose of auction fever.

Buyers, too, get in on the act whenever they solicit multiple bids from professional service providers (e.g., accountants, building contractors, office cleaners, messenger services, etc.). Essentially, they're contriving an auction in reverse. If our facility manager in London asks four companies to bid on our office maintenance contract, the competition he's created instantly increases our value as a customer. It reminds the bidders that even though there are thousands of companies in London, legitimate customers like us for their particular service are hard to find—and there will be one less customer in their universe if they let us slip away to a competitor. Even in the mundane world of office maintenance, the reverse auction imbues us with rarity and, hence, value. If our facility manager orchestrates the bidding properly, the bidders will not only lower their price for our contract, but they will actually tell us what should and shouldn't be in the contract. A seller competing for a customer will not only tell you what's right with him but what's wrong with the other guys. In effect, when we pool their collective arguments, we find that they are literally teaching us how to negotiate with them.

Auctions are standard procedure for people who sell rare things, whether they are fine art or antiques or Thoroughbred horses or intellectual properties such as a novel or movie script. Auctions happen to be a valuable negotiating tool in parts of our business, particularly in the area of television rights. After all, there is only one event like Wimbledon or the Olympic Games. Negotiating the sale of the broadcast rights to these unique properties demands an auction process.

I realize few people negotiate for world-class sports properties, but the methods we've employed and the lessons we've learned in that area can help anyone construct a bidding process that maximizes the suspense and competitive fever. The following three lessons, applied with grace and from a position of strength, will always attract the best price for your product or service.

1. SPELL OUT EXACTLY WHAT'S FOR SALE.

The more aspects of the auction you control, the more leverage you have over the bidders.

When we auction off the broadcast rights to a major sports event among three or more competing television networks, we like to grab total control of the process at the start. We can do this with one simple gesture: We draft an exhaustive contract that spells out everything the networks would be bidding on, from camera positions to the number of hotel rooms allotted for network staff at the event to ownership of the videotapes to how the event's logo can and cannot be used in advertising. Every deal point is included in this document *except price*. We then submit the contract to all the networks and ask them to sign the documents, leaving the monetary elements blank, to indicate their acceptance of all the nonmonetary provisions. They have to sign to qualify to bid for the event.

This gambit takes advantage of a paradox that too many negotiators overlook:

- If you agree to a specific price, the *other side* wins all the other deal points.

- If the other side agrees to all the nonmonetary deal points, *you* win on price.

In this case, by agreeing in writing to all our provisions, the networks lose their ability to haggle over our terms in order to reduce the cost of the deal. If and when the bidding reaches an uncomfortably high level, we don't want the networks suddenly backpedaling and saying, "Wait a minute. If you take out these three provisions, we can afford it." We like to think we are auctioning one take-it-or-leave-it broadcasting package, not an "economy" versus a "luxury" version.

That's a great position to be in. The networks help put us there the moment they sign our contract.

2. Add a little theater.

I've already discussed the myth of the negotiating table and the importance of conducting negotiations in congenial quasi-social settings. That's even more important in an auction, which is by definition a dramatic situation. Controlling location and ambiance can heighten the drama and the bids.

Whenever possible, we try to lure the bidders to a neutral (but attractive) location. On major negotiations, we have found that it's smart to get the bidding parties out of their offices, to get them away from the phones, the second-guessers, and the bosses who could distract them or make them lose their ardor for our property. If you force people to travel a long distance, the trip itself is a major investment of time, which intensifies their commitment. If you bring people to a relaxed and beautiful locale, the occasion almost seems like a vacation. And we all know people tend to spend more on vacation.

3. KEEP THE CLOCK TICKING.

A master auctioneer selling Impressionist masterpieces at Sotheby's knows how to control the pace and rhythm in the room to escalate the bidding. If he's in tune with the interested parties, he can quicken his pace so that even experienced bidders get caught up in the frenzy and bid higher than they intended. The rush makes them afraid the bidding will pass them by.

The "conduct of the auction"—pushing the right buttons and being willing to change course as the auction unfolds—is the finesse part of auctioneering that escapes many people.

Again, the advantage is all with the auctioneer, because he or she is the one setting the ground rules.

In my experience with sports properties, auctions go better when they go quickly. We don't want a sense of calm or, worse, dull lethargy to dampen the proceedings. We don't want to give the bidding parties too much time to think between bids. We want them to feel that, at any moment, the property on the block could slip away.

So we keep the ground rules simple but pay strict attention to the clock. In one auction a few years ago, we gathered representatives from three American networks at a resort in Scotland to bid on a major event. Each network had agreed to our terms for the auction and signed a contract. Only the price was left blank.

We hosted a dinner party for the combatants the night before the auction to maintain the congenial air. The next morning, after a hearty Scottish breakfast, the auction began with each network submitting blind bids in sealed envelopes. Under the ground rules, after the opening bids, we would get back to the networks with the figures within 15 minutes. As long as the underbidders were within 10 percent of the top bid, they were still in the game. The networks then had 30 minutes to come back with a second bid. This went on through nine rounds, with each network gently bumping up its bid by 5 to 10 percent, hoping to stay within 10 percent of the top bid.

To a disinterested party watching the proceedings in our meeting room, this auction must have seemed a dull affair—like watching paint dry. But I doubt if the network negotiators thought it was dull. With millions of dollars at stake and the 30-minute clock hanging over their heads as they tried to calculate bids that knocked out the competition but didn't break the bank, I suspect time went by very quickly for them.

For our part, we knew that each new round of bidding meant more money for our client. That's exciting. In the end, after nine rounds, the winning network had more than doubled its opening bid and exceeded our in-house estimate by 50 percent.

That sort of result is almost predictable when you consider the contract we got the networks to sign, the seductive setting we placed them in, and the bidding pace we established. Quite honestly, the networks never really had a chance.

• • •
THE MCCORMACK RULES

- There seems to be an unwritten code that the people who initiated the deal are the ones who close the deal. They stay in the game even if they are no longer effective. My advice: Question the code.

- Injecting new people into the mix is the best solution to a negotiating impasse, but only if these new people are in the room to cooperate, not argue.

- A well-timed wisecrack can puncture the tensions and pretensions of any impasse. But you have to be bold, blunt, and quick to pull it off.

- To play hardball in business you need an influential third party to keep everyone at the table. Without that third party influencing the situation, you're not playing hardball, you're just making it hard to get things done.

- When the other side puts a gun to your head, act as if the gun isn't loaded.

- If the buyer meets or exceeds your price and you have the nagging feeling that you can get a little more, keep it to yourself.

- Never go into a negotiation without knowing exactly how much you are willing to concede. Conceding a negotiating point is a golden opportunity to get something greater in return.

- You are under no obligation to tell the other side that a concession is easy to make or immaterial to you. And you don't have to concede immediately.

- The paradox of long-term relationships is that to maintain them, you have to spend as much time protecting yourself from success as you do from failure.

- When you shut out the competition *and* get the other side to make the first offer, you have every right to feel you're getting a bargain.

- An auction is negotiating taken to its most sophisticated (and exciting) extreme. Not everyone can do it.

CHAPTER 7

What's Your
Negotiating IQ?

N ow let's see what you've learned. The following hypotheticals cover some of the thornier negotiating issues.

DESPERATE DEAL OR NONE AT ALL

Q: People who are desperate to get a deal done tend to give up more than they should. Their desperation forces them into bad or mediocre deals. (See "What You Can Learn from Negotiating with Your Spouse" in chapter 2.) But not everyone has the luxury of being able to walk away from a mediocre deal—even though they know it's mediocre. If there were no other options, which would you choose: a desperate deal or no deal at all?

A: My first impulse is to go with the desperate deal, but not for the obvious reason that you *might* be able to make it work out. My real reason: It's a valuable learning experience. But I would not recommend it twice. You only have to get locked into a bad deal once to appreciate the wisdom of walking away when things don't sound right.

For an example that hits close to home to anyone in business, just think about the last time you hired someone because you were desperate to fill a position rather than wait for a candidate with the right credentials. How much money, time, and grief did that "desperate deal" cost you?

The correct answer is "no deal." No matter how desperate things look when the customer in front of you threatens to disappear unless you accept his or her terms, the wise response is to let it pass. There will always be another customer. Also, if you stick to your guns, you stand a decent chance of turning around an unreasonable prospect. If you cave in, you'll never know if you could have done better.

THE WRONG SWITCH

Q: You recently switched jobs, only to learn that the "perfect spot" was really a dead spot. Your new employer totally misrepresented how much drudge work and how little responsibility and chance for advancement you would have. What's your next move?

A: Perhaps some employers regard this as corporate justice for all those applicants who totally misrepresent *their* credentials. But that's not fair to you.

It's also small comfort to know you're not the first to fall for this corporate bait-and-switch. It happens at all levels. I've known CEOs who switched executive suites only to find that their new company was in far worse shape than they were told or that the chairman of the board was not as "retiring" as they were led to believe.

You're in a no-win situation. Start looking for another job. And next time, if possible, do three things: (1) negotiate your responsibilities before you come on board; (2) get any agreements with your boss in writing (this doesn't have to be an employment contract, but it's just as good); and (3) find out what happened to your predecessor.

No More Free Milk

Q: For several years you have been giving speeches—with your company's blessing—on economic trends to professional groups. You have never received a fee for doing so. You're now working for yourself. You would like to get paid for your time. Several groups that have invited you back each year are balking at a fee. "Why pay for the cow when you can get the milk for free?" is their attitude. How would you convince them that you're worth the money?

A: Start with the assumption that the repeat invitations mean they like what you have to say. Then stick to your rate card. Your changed circumstance (the fact that you're working for yourself) is the best reason to introduce a change in your price.

The easiest way to break down price resistance, however, is to offer a "money-back guarantee." If your host doesn't feel your appearance fully justified your fee, tell him you'll give it back.

This is a clever gambit when it comes to personal services. If you're confident about your ability to wow an audience, this shouldn't cost you anything. You really have to fail badly for people to ask for their money back. It also reduces your host's risk to nothing if he feels he's not getting his money's worth. More important, in paying you, the host is making a tacit admission that you were good. That may be the perfect moment for you to offer your services to the same group next year, preferably at your current rate, before you increase it. Who knows? In a few years they may think your fee is a bargain.

COMPETITION HELPS

Q: Your boss recently killed the "deal of the year" for you because he or she thought you were selling too low. The buyer wouldn't budge on price and ultimately went to one of your competitors, who made a huge success out of "your deal." How do you convince your boss to trust you the next time?

A: There are all sorts of reason to make a sale at what looks like a loss-leader price.

You want to get your foot in the door with a new customer.

You need the gross volume to keep your operations running at full capacity.

You want to enter a new area and the lowball price is the entry fee.

Your people can learn new skills by rubbing shoulders with the new customer.

You want the customer's prestigious name on your customer list.

But you had what is usually the strongest reason to cut your price: to stop the competition from getting the business. This is the argument you should have been using all along.

You can blame your boss for missing this point once, but blame yourself if he or she misses it again.

REFUND, PLEASE

Q: A project you handled for a major customer turned out badly—not because of anything you did but because of an error made by one of the customer's regular suppliers. Yet the customer holds you responsible. The supplier's error put the project $35,000 over budget and the customer expects you to foot that bill. Do you hold your ground or give in to keep this major account happy?

A: First of all, assume the issue here isn't money. The real issue is your competence and professionalism. Cutting a check for the $35,000 may momentarily soothe a big customer you *think* you can't afford to irritate.

But what about the long-term impact on your reputation? No matter how you rationalize it, that check is still an admission of guilt, of incompetence, proof that somewhere along the line you dropped the ball. Before I would reimburse someone for a mistake I didn't commit, I would go to extraordinary lengths to establish exactly who did.

Of course, once you have cleared your name with the customer, the matter doesn't end there. The customer is still looking for "satisfaction." The ideal solution is to make the real culprit—the incompetent supplier—pay.

But it's not a bad idea to *offer* to make the customer whole.

There's no way to predict whether a reasonable customer, who knows you weren't at fault, will accept or decline your offer. But I guarantee you the customer will be impressed by it. The gesture is not unlike a restaurateur tearing up the check when you complain that the meal or the service was uncommonly disappointing. The torn bill won't save your meal that day, but it seems to cement the relationship between you and the restaurant—and ensures that you will come back another day.

AN AGENT FOR YOU

Q: You are about to switch jobs. Should you have someone represent you in negotiating the terms of your new employment? Or are you better off handling the negotiation yourself?

A: It depends on the complexity of the job and the amount of money involved. At the most senior levels, having representation for an employment agreement is fairly common.

But even at the middle-management level, having a third party involved is sometimes not a bad idea. People get distracted by the euphoria that usually comes with a new job offer. A third party adds two features to the equation:

- **A third party can look at considerations that bring the new opportunity back down to earth.**

- A third party is more comfortable discussing the terms of your departure should things go wrong (which seems to be very important nowadays at the highest corporate level).

Having said that, I should point out that as an employer myself I would resent the presence of an "agent." I would always think that, no matter how fair I was, the agent would be trying to improve the deal simply to justify his own fee.

To avoid antagonizing your new employer, have your agent consult you from *behind the scenes*. No one needs to know that you're being advised—and you will certainly be the wiser for it.

HOLDING GROUND

Q: You are in the middle of a long and tense negotiation when suddenly your counterpart across the table loses his cool and becomes extremely obnoxious. He attacks you—unfairly—for drafting an agreement that, in his view, contains some "trick clauses." You can respond in kind, but that might destroy the relationship. How do you hold your ground so you can live to negotiate another day?

A: My first impulse would be to *blame someone else* for the drafting errors. If the other side is angry about the terms of a draft contract, blame it on the lawyers. Say "I was out of town and the lawyers messed up. You know how they are. I agree with you." That may mollify an angry adversary.

My second impulse, however, would be to ask myself, "Is this person out of control, or is he using his anger tactically to make *me* lose control?"

I know one wealthy sports entrepreneur who has an arsenal of negotiating tactics. Depending on his motives, he can wear you down, outlast you, ignore you, or confuse you.

But his favorite tactic, I think, is to outshout you. He has been known to burst into offices in a volcanic rage when transactions aren't going his way—because he knows most people will be intimidated by this behavior and cave in.

The appropriate response to such rage, of course, is to keep your cool and stand your ground. As a general rule, the louder they get, the quieter you should get.

FIRST DRAFT

Q: You've just agreed on a deal. Who writes the first draft of the contract?

A: Given the choice, you should write the first draft. That way, the other side is working with your words rather than vice versa.

Of course, you don't always have the choice. If you do business with government agencies, you can be sure that you will be using their forms. Likewise with large corporate bureaucracies. Lawyers at the television networks, for example, have fairly rigid ideas about what goes into a contract and always insist on drafting it.

There are times when you may actually want the other side to write the first draft, particularly if they are more experienced or knowledgeable about the deal than you are. It not only saves time but can be a learning experience for you. It may bring to the surface items and clauses that you would never have considered—and that you can insert into future agreements.

BACK TO THE BEGINNING

Q: For years your company has been buying your materials from the same supplier. When you started with him, the supplier had the most competitive pricing and great service. His service is still great, but over time his prices have crept up to the point where they're not so competitive. You would like to keep this supplier. How would you negotiate him back to the good old days when his was the best price in town?

A: The good news is that you're already halfway there—simply by noticing that your supplier's prices are no longer a bargain. It's amazing how many companies overlook this. A lazy inertia settles over customers when they are happy with a vendor. Once they find the lowest-cost supplier, they think they never have to worry about that purchasing category again. They don't notice that the annual 5 percent or 10 percent price increases over the course of a few years ultimately push the vendor into premium-price territory.

Your negotiating strategy is simple: Find another vendor willing to undercut your current supplier's prices. If a friendly discussion with your supplier won't convince him to roll back his prices, the specter of one or two competitors most certainly will.

If you think that this sort of give-back negotiation will affect your personal relationship with the supplier, blame it on a new corporate policy—the one where your company requires at least three competitive bids on every major purchase.

Frankly, competitive bidding is what you should have been doing all along.

BLAME THE POLICY

Q: You represent busy, talented clients who develop food products and marketing concepts for most of the major manufacturers in the United States. From time to time, because of deadline pressures and the unavailability of a client, you have been forced to sign a contract on behalf of your client. You know this is stupid because it makes you responsible for something out of your control, namely your client's performance of the terms in the contract. But when a big customer is lighting matches under your toes to get the deal done, you feel you don't have a choice. How do you serve your clients while at the same time protecting yourself?

A: Again, blame it on the policy.

At IMG, we have an ironclad policy that says clients sign their own contracts. We think it's extremely important that a client has the chance to review any agreement requiring his or her time, services, name, or image before it is executed, and the only way to verify the client has seen it is to have him or her sign it. I'm not sure other representatives think along the same lines, but we see ourselves strictly as an agent, not a principal, in any transaction.

It's a crucial distinction, but I can see how people lose sight of it. If you've spent months courting a customer and pitching ideas, and one day he or she bites at an idea, there's nothing more gratifying than being able to say, "You have a deal!"

But you don't really have the power to say that. You've overstepped your authority. And you may be setting yourself up for a fall if the client says no to a deal you led the customer to believe was a *fait accompli.* There's nothing more embarrassing than having to go back to the customer and say, "We don't have a deal yet."

When the customer bites, you're far better off saying, "Subject to my client's approval, you have a deal." I don't see how that simple response does any damage to your credibility or ego.

The more worrisome problem here are the big customers "lighting matches under your toes." Don't let the other side pressure you into hasty agreements. You should always be wondering—privately and out loud—why the other side is in such a hurry. In my experience, there are very few deals, if any, that cannot wait a few days while you track down the client to go over the agreement. Unless you know something specific about the transaction, a deal that looks good on Monday usually doesn't fall apart because the documents didn't get signed until Thursday.

ONE TOUGH COOKIE DESERVES ANOTHER

Q: You are about to go into a series of negotiations with a gentleman who has a fearsome reputation for being very pigheaded and tough. How would you deal with this alleged tough cookie?

A: First, you have to determine whether this man is as tough as advertised. Is he belligerent and difficult with everyone? Or is he merely a bully who only picks fights he knows he can win?

The answer to that question will instruct you how to proceed.

As a general rule, bullies are simple to deal with. But you must be prepared to confront them early on.

I recall meeting with a notoriously difficult Japanese television executive whose dislike for sports in general and disdain for sports people in particular was well known. But he realized sports was an essential part of his broadcasting schedule and he needed our help. Still, the meeting took eight months to arrange. People in our company reminded me of the man's reputation and advised me to be extremely deferential with him.

However, I took the opposite tack. From everything I heard about him, he sounded like a classic bully—someone who was used to getting his own way because no one dared oppose him. From the start, I was confrontational, telling him all the mistakes his company had made over the years and how these could have been avoided if he had come to us sooner.

He protested that people didn't usually talk to him this way. But I could tell I had made a strong impression because the discussion that followed was cordial, rational, and productive. It would be nice to report that we walked away from the table that day as bosom buddies and business partners, but that's asking too much of one meeting. It took a half-dozen more meetings (all more easily arranged than the first) before our companies began working together.

Going against the prevailing wisdom also works when you are dealing with genuinely difficult people.

The normal impulse in handling tough cookies is to try to match them every step of the way. When they push, you push back harder. Backing down is a sign of weakness. The goal is to make the other guy blink.

In my experience, this is patently silly.

Several years ago I spent a golf weekend with the CEO of an electronics conglomerate. He did not like sports agents at all. Because of that, he was very difficult to deal with and had shunned our company for years. But he and I were thrust together for three days in Scotland, so I decided to make the most of it.

I played the role of Mr. Nice Guy. I didn't talk business. I complimented his golf game. I solicited his advice on certain shots. When the conversation turned to our business, I steered it back so I could learn more about him and his company. Everything was designed to make him feel important and to change his opinion about agents. Not surprisingly, it worked. That weekend helped us forge a sensational relationship— and a short time later our companies began working together.

Keep both of these examples in mind in your negotiation. If your opponent is as tough as people say, you'll do much better by deferring to him or her. If he or she is all bark and no bite, there's a good chance he or she won't be ready when you pounce.

THE LAST WALTZ

Q: You have been waltzing around an agreement with a new customer for weeks. But every time you get the customer's negotiating team to resolve a point, they bring up two more to fight over. How do you break this negotiating stalemate?

A: First option: Take a break from each other. Someone, hopefully the other side, will become more flexible during this cooling-off period. Of course, you run the risk of losing the customer altogether during the break.

A much better strategy: Offer to change one or more members of the negotiating team. And ask them to do the same. Or change your team makeup without announcing it. There seems to be an unwritten rule in negotiating that the players who start the game are expected to finish it. But that's foolish. If you were a soccer coach, you wouldn't stick with a goalie who couldn't block a shot. You would bring in replacements.

It's the same with any business transaction. Putting new faces into the picture may produce a totally different look in the final agreement. At the very least, the new teams will do no worse than the current set of negotiators.

CONTROLLING FEES

Q: Legal fees at your company have gone through the roof. How can you control them?

A: Your first move requires an attitude adjustment about lawyers. Some executives regard attorneys as their best friend and protection. They feel that having their attorney next to them is like having the Terminator on their side. It gives them confidence to do bold and legally risky things.

I don't. I regard each business day in which I never have to deal with a legal matter or a lawyer (whose meter, remember, is always running) as a personal victory. To stop soaring legal costs, you must first stop thinking of lawyers as personal accessories and start thinking of them as very expensive specialists who represent your last, not your first, resort.

The second step is simple. Don't sue. There are more ways to settle a dispute than letting a lawyer do it. A lot of the solutions may require you to write a check to the other side, but that check is usually much smaller than the one you'll have to give to your lawyer.

The third step, when all else fails and you cannot avoid hiring an attorney, is reminding yourself that *everything is negotiable*. Lawyers (and doctors) want you to believe they are exempt from this rule. But it's not true. There is a glut of attorneys today. The laws of supply and demand should tell you that it's a buyer's market.

Lawyers won't volunteer that their hourly rates are negotiable. So you must ask: Will they reduce their hourly rate? Will they put a cap on the total hours they bill for the case? Will they accept a flat fee? Will they accept a multitiered fee, depending on the outcome? Will they barter their time for your company's services or products? You'd be amazed how quickly attorneys agree to some or all of these suggestions.

THE TELLTALE CLUE

Q: There's one clue that tells you when you're dealing with a skilled negotiator or a neophyte. What is it?

A: The answer: How the other side deals with silence. A pro talks only when it improves the silence. An amateur talks too much, presumably to fill the vacuum created by silence. If you want a quick assessment of the opposition, just sit there and say nothing. You'll have your answer in seconds.

GET YOUR RAISE

Q: You think you deserve a raise. How do you go about getting it?

A: The best strategy, though hardly the only one, is: Think of others before you think about yourself.

In most companies, salaries do not exist in a vacuum. They are carefully determined in relation to everyone else. For example, if your assistant makes $25,000, you make $50,000, and your boss makes $75,000, a big raise for you will upset that delicate balance. Your assistant will feel cheated and your boss will feel threatened.

If you can first get an increase for your assistant and help your boss earn more, your raise is a foregone conclusion. You are far more likely to increase your compensation after you've increased everyone else's stake as well.

THE IDEAL DEAL

Q: How do you define a great deal?

A: A great deal is when you get the right price—and yet the other party doesn't feel that they've lost.

A great deal is when you don't get delayed or depressed or destroyed during the specifics of the negotiation phase—that is, you don't give away too much of your "right" price in order to get the deal done.

A great deal is the moment when all the contracts are signed and money changes hands—and both parties are still smiling.

Index